one step forward

THe STORY OF
TeaCHaiTi's SCHOOL OF HOPe

BY LYNN HUMMEL
WITH assistance FROM JeFF NORBY

One Step Forward
The Story of TeacHaiti's School of Hope

ISBN: 978-0-692-22263-8

Printed in the United States of America

CONTENTS

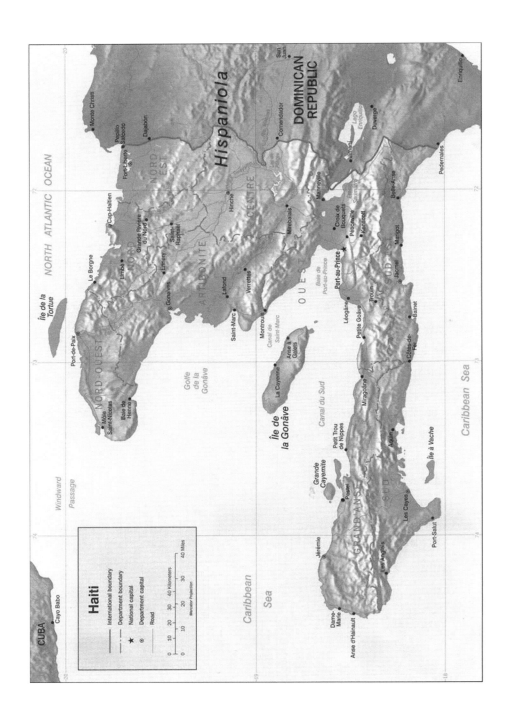

4

One Step Forward

August, 2002. Miquette Denie, a 22 year old exchange student from Haiti, who begin the first exercise in an orientation program for international students. It was a get-acquainted drill. Who are you? What is your background? How did you get here? A group of about 25 new students, all wearing their yellow freshman beanies, were directed to stand in a straight line. They were all asked a series of questions and requested to take one step forward for each yes answer. Some of the questions:
Step forward if you lived with your mother and father. The shy freshman stepped forward. That was to be her only step forward.

- Step forward if you had electricity in your home.
- Step forward if your family had a refrigerator.
- Step forward if there was enough food for you and your family.
- Step forward if you had your own room.
- Step forward if you had a television in your home.
- Step forward if your parents took a vacation with you.
- Step forward if you ever had a birthday party.
- Step forward if your parents had a high school education.
  Step forward if your parents had a college education.
  Step forward if your parents had a PhD or professional degree.

There were more questions, but Miquette never moved beyond step one. Most of her classmates made all the steps except the one about PhD or professional degree. Some stopped short of that mark.

PREFACE

On that date, Miquette Denie was one of the great natural resources of Haiti, its people. Only she didn't know it and neither did anybody else, though a few may have suspected as much.

This book will sketch a brief history of Haiti from the time of Columbus to the present day—a heartbreaking history of exploitation, slavery, political chaos, dictators, murder, torture, exploitation of Haitians by Haitians, greed, hunger, poverty, disease, illiteracy and economic and natural disasters, climaxed by the horrific earthquake of January, 2010.

You will learn about Miquette Denie, now Miquette Denie McMahon, where she grew up, how her family had to maintain two homes, miles apart, in order to try to feed all the children. You will be told about her struggle to be educated, with interruptions due to lack of funds. You will learn that five of her siblings spent time in orphanages because there simply was not enough food at home to feed them. Three of those children were surrendered to adoption. One to a family in Canada and two to a family in Detroit Lakes, Minnesota. Ten years later, that Detroit Lakes family brought Miquette, an awkward 20 year old high school junior, to their home as a Rotary exchange student. There she would live with the family that included two sisters who were strangers to her. You will follow Miquette through her last two years of high school, the final one at Oak Grove Lutheran High School in Fargo, North Dakota and four years at Concordia College to earn a nursing degree in 2007.

The year following her graduation, Miquette took her nursing boards and worked as a nurse at St. Mary's Hospital and Emmanuel Nursing Home in

Detroit Lakes. It was during this period that her dreams and visions came into focus. She would solicit support from her friends and co-workers to raise enough money for scholarships for 10 poor Haitian children who, because of the almost total absence of public schools in Haiti, would not learn to read or write without financial support to pay tuition in private schools. Her vision became her passion and before she left the United States to return to her homeland, TeacHaiti was born as a non-profit organization, a board of directors was elected, then Miquette returned to Haiti as a nurse and teacher with enough money for tuition for 41 children.

The program grew each year until January, 2010 when the ground shook in Port au Prince and many of those private schools were reduced to rubble. Where would the TeacHaiti children go now? It was soon decided that TeacHaiti would open its own school in addition to continuing the sponsorship of children in other private schools. A little building was leased, painted, remodeled, furnished with books and school supplies and opened in September, 2010 with grades 1-4. This was the School of Hope. You will learn more about the School of Hope, its philosophy, its administration, its faculty (Haitians working for Haitians), its students, their parents and its plans for growth and expansion.

Haiti needs a stable government, streets, roads, bridges, a rebuilt economy, better health care and educated children and adults. TeacHaiti doesn't build streets, roads or bridges, but educating children and building citizens is the beginning of the search for the light at the end of the tunnel. In One Step Forward, The Story of TeacHaiti School of Hope, you will learn of this crusade—and you may wish to join it.

CHAPTER 1

I CAN'T FEED MY CHILDREN

"There are people in the world so hungry, that God cannot appear to them except in the form of bread."

—Mahatma Ghandi

Where does this story begin? There are probably four heroes in this book, people without whom there would be no TeacHaiti School of Hope story to tell. Miquette Denie, of course, is one of them, John and Mary Lee are two more and Rose Denie, Miquette's mother, is the fourth and least conspicuous. Rose is, and always has been the CEO of the Denie family.

Rose and her husband Cleuis had nine children. Two died and seven are still living. The family started in St. Michel, a village in northern Haiti on the Central Plateau, and life was grim. Cleuis was working as a carpenter and Rose was working as a cook at the school Miquette attended (on and off) for $1.50 a week. She was also working at the local hospital doing laundry for $2.00 a week. The family had to pay $2.00 per month to keep Miquette in school, but she was sent home one week because the family was $1.50 short on her tuition payment. Cleuis might earn $5.00 or $6.00 in a good week for roofing a house, but sometimes $1.00 was all he made in a week.

In 1987, it became obvious something had to change. The family wasn't making it. So Rose got on a truck box with a truck load of "refugees" and headed 150 miles south for Port au Prince to find employment. None of the children came except Sandra, but she didn't live with Rose, she lived with an aunt. Daughter Beatrice was already working at Cap Haitian. Rose had no job and no place to stay. She was desperate. But she had an idea. Gladys Sylvestre had once lived in St. Michel and she was running a guest house for missionaries in Port au Prince. Rose contacted Gladys and got a job cooking and cleaning at the guest house. The wages weren't much better than St. Michel, only $5.00 a week plus room and board. But, unknown to Gladys, Rose sometimes got tips from the missionaries. She worked for Gladys at the guest house for five years.

Back in St. Michel, Rose's family was moving to Port au Prince one member at a time. In 1990, her son Pidens came. Two years later, Isaac followed. The last child left, Miquette, made the move with her dad, Cleuis, at the age of 15 in 1995.

Rose saved her money while working and purchased a lot and built a one room house. Then she left Gladys and spent a year without a job. During that time she became a street merchant, as her mother had been back in St. Michel. She sold spices, onions, garlic and cooking supplies.

By this time, Gladys Sylvestre, a true entrepreneur, was also operating an orphanage for special needs children. Gladys called Rose and offered her a job at the orphanage for $40 a month. The job did not involve cooking or cleaning; it was a child-care job. She cared for physically and developmentally delayed children and adults, feeding them, cleaning their messes, lifting them in and out of bed, lifting them in and out of their wheelchairs—heavy physical work. When Miquette later came to Port au Prince, she worked at the orphanage part time at age 16, doing all the same things her mother was doing. She never got more than $50.00 a month. Rose developed back and shoulder problems after 17 years at the orphanage. Later, when Miquette was in America, she sent money home and Rose's daughter, Sandra, encouraged her mother to quit.

After Rose left the orphanage, she set up shop in her own home, selling the same cooking and household supplies. Much of what she sold in Port au Prince she purchased in St. Michel. She rode back and forth in big open-box trucks packed with people, bags of produce, mattresses and luggage bags. The roads between Port au Prince and St. Michel were very rough and treacherous in those days (still rough and treacherous in 2013 as observed by this writer—also 10 river crossings—in the water, without bridges). She was involved in three accidents. In the last one a heavy sack landed on her ear, puncturing an ear drum.

In 1986, Rose's daughter, Beatrice, age 16, gave birth to Cherline. Rose cared for Cherline as her own daughter from day one. Caring for Cherline and Farah, only eight months older, was impossible and unhealthy. There wasn't enough food to go around. By the time Cherline was two it became obvious that the girls would have to be surrendered. The decision to give them up had to be the most difficult decision Rose and Cleuis ever made. The orphanage helped Rose "fix" Cherline's birth certificate to record Rose as her mother. Rose, who couldn't read or write at that time, signed with an "X." Cleuis didn't have to sign at all. Beatrice's name didn't appear anywhere in the records. Gladys had two orphanages, one for handicapped and children with special needs and one for "regular" orphans who were adoptable. The girls were in the latter institution. Their big brother, Isaac, had stayed with his sisters every day when he came home from school. One day he came home and they were gone. Nobody had told Isaac about leaving his sisters at the orphanage. Isaac cried.

Rose expected relief when the children were placed, but it was not to be. Adoptive parents were unknown at that time and the outlook for the children appeared to be an entire childhood in the orphanage. When Rose visited them, the children cried and clung to her. It was heartbreaking for all of them. Rose wanted to take them back but it was impossible. After a year in the orphanage, adoptive parents were found, and the children were flown away to be adopted by strangers in a foreign country. Rose could not bear to go to the airport to see them off. She knew she would never see them again. Rose prayed earnestly that the girls would find a good home.

CHAPTER 2

WANTED: TWO LITTLE GIRLS

*"Bring My Sons From Afar And My Daughters
From The Ends Of The Earth."*

—Isaiah 43:6

In Detroit Lakes, Minnesota, USA, exactly 2,387 miles north of Port au Prince, Haiti, Rev. John and Mary Lee had two children, both sons, Daniel, age 8 ½ and Carl, age 6 ½. They believed in zero population growth but they wanted two girls. How do you get more children without adding to the population of the world? You adopt them. But, not so simple—John was 40 and Mary was 38. John and Mary had worked previously with Lutheran Social Services regarding adoptions and knew the age limit for adoptive parents was 35. Besides, LSS had a long waiting list for adoptions.

Not to be discouraged, they kept looking. Mary saw a newspaper ad by the Building Families Through Adoption Agency in Dassel, Minnesota and noted that the non-profit had scheduled an adoption seminar in Bemidji, Minnesota, 90 miles away. Mary went to the seminar and learned that the children of Haiti were available for adoption in great numbers. Further, she discovered that the waiting period for Haitian children was typically about one year, compared to 4-5 years for Korean children (less for others depending on home studies and processing), that it was possible to adopt more than one child at a time and that the parents didn't have to travel to Haiti to get the children (that was changed later).

Of course the children of Haiti are black. That was no problem for the Lees. John had spent a half year at the 97% black Virginia Union University as an exchange student in his second year of college while he was attending Concordia College in Moorhead, Minnesota. As part of that experience, he spent his 20th birthday listening to Malcolm X tapes among 200 students who had occupied the VUU administrative building. Further, he was traveling through Baltimore, Maryland, with black friends in 1968 when Martin Luther King was assassinated. He was gaining insight into the black world and culture, including food, music and even jive talk. Later, as a pastoral intern at Luther Seminary, he had worked in the Native American culture in the Bagley, Minnesota area. Mary Lee grew up in Madison, Wisconsin and studied physical therapy, then nursing at the multi-cultural University of Wisconsin. During the summers she had worked as a counselor in a camp for inner city girls from Chicago and had worked with many African American girls. Black children would not be a problem for the Lees.

After Mary returned from the adoption seminar in Bemidji, the Lees petitioned to start the adoption process through the Foundation for the Children of Haiti. It was their preference that the girls would be preschoolers in their formative years, 2-5 years old, younger sisters in logical birth order behind Daniel and Carl.

The Lees and their sons were interviewed, they had home visits, they were checked out at John Lee's pastorage for the Lund, Bakke and Richwood parishes and they successfully completed and survived the required home study and waited to hear about children becoming available to them. They got a call: three children, girl–boy–girl, were ready to be placed. The oldest of these children was older than Carl. This presented a scary decision for the family: three kids, another boy, scrambled birth order—they pondered and prayed, then decided not to take the three. More waiting.

Their next call was just what they were waiting for: two sisters, less than a year apart, age 3 and almost 4. They got only one picture of the girls, both in clean white dresses (made available for the picture only, then returned to the orphanage where the picture was taken), one named Cherline in the arms of her glum mother, Rose Denie, and one, named Farah, standing beside her mother. The girls had been born in a home with a dirt floor in St. Michel, Haiti, to a family that already had nine children, but two had died. One of their sisters was Miquette, five years older than Farah. The family had nothing. The youngest children were running around on the streets, sometimes naked, and their parents had simply decided they would have to take painful, drastic steps to survive.

The Lees were required to send airplane tickets for these two daughters-to-be they had never set their eyes on, fare for a travel escort, and clothes for the girls for traveling. In all, the adoption cost them $12,000. They sent more than enough clothes they had picked up at garage sales, cute, colorful clothes. They still have the dresses the girls were wearing when they arrived at the Minneapolis Airport on June 22, 1989. Many Haitian children were on that flight and Mary recognized some of the clothes she had sent on other children. Cherline was 3 years old plus a few weeks and Farah was 3 years, 8 months. They were tiny. Cherline weighed 27 pounds and Farah was 29 pounds.

The Lees took the girls to the dentist and doctor the next day and found there were problems that needed care. The girls were scared and reserved, but not too scared and reserved to eat. Because of the fear since their first days of not having enough to eat, they ate anything, everything and too much when they arrived in the land of plenty. They had never been full before, and to start with, they didn't stop until it hurt. Drumsticks were gnawed down until nothing was left but dry bone.

There was confusion almost immediately about the ages of the girls and their birth certificates. They weren't even nine months apart. In October, the Lees wrote to Gladys Sylvestre, manager of the orphanage and home for the handicapped in Port au Prince, asking for clarification and details. Sylvestre wrote back with an explanation. It turned out that Cherline was the daughter of Beatrice, 16, one of Rose's older children, born out of wedlock, but being raised as a daughter of Rose and Cleuis. The only way an adoption of both children could have been achieved was for Rose to sign that both were her daughters and that she was surrendering them due to poverty. Interestingly, no consent by Cleuis was required and Beatrice was never recorded as being the mother of Cherline. Would any other country than Haiti have these huge blank spaces in the records of its citizens?

At Christmas time that year and every year since, the Lees have sent a letter with pictures of the girls to Gladys Sylvestre at the orphanage with the request that they be shared with Rose. Because Rose was working at the orphanage with Gladys, she received the pictures and annual updates about her children's lives in the United States.

Other families in Minnesota had adopted children from Haiti through the same agency and the families communicated with one another and had meetings from time to time. They formed a "Haiti Camp" and sent money to Gladys to have Gladys fly to Minnesota each summer beginning in 1991 to see the children and meet with their families. When Gladys came she brought pictures of Cherline's mother (Farah's sister), Beatrice, and they also brought pictures of Farah's older sister (and Cherline's aunt), Miquette.

Over the years the Lees learned more and more about Miquette. Farah, Cherline, Daniel, Carl, John and Mary Lee all adapted to the new family situation and all went well.

CHAPTER 3

TEN YEARS LATER

"The family is one of nature's masterpieces."
—George Santayana

Ten years later, in 1999, John, then in his fifteenth year of ministry in the Bakke-Lund-Richwood Lutheran Parish, was offered a three month sabbatical leave. He elected to spend one month of the leave, May, in Haiti to do mission work and attempt to meet the Haitian family of Farah and Cherline.

By this time, it was required that families wishing to adopt Haitian children must come to Haiti to get them. In order to help expedite this process, Gladys Sylvestre, manager of the orphanage, had established a guest house for the prospective adoptive parents and others in Haiti to do mission work. John Lee stayed at the guest house and did general handyman jobs to support the program.

While he was in Haiti, Lee saw a play at a chapel called "Culture Shock," about what it was like for Americans in Haiti. Everything was different: climate, diet, language, and culture. And of course, it was a reminder to him of the culture shock experienced by Farah and Cherline when they came to America.

Later, John went to the orphanage/handicap home seeking to meet Rose, remembering roughly what she looked like based on the single picture of her with the two girls he had seen 10 years earlier. He was directed to a woman named Rose at the home and knew immediately she couldn't have been the Rose he was looking for because this one was twice the size of the girls' mother. John continued his search.

Later that same day, Lee was back at the guest house. There was a tapping at the gate. Two women were looking for him. The younger one, in broken English, said "This is Rose and I'm from Miquette." Miquette was then 18, almost 19, but was still, after many interruptions in her stop-and-go educational path, only a 10th grader. This discussion, burdened by language differences, did not go well and Miquette suggested they get a neighbor, Carmel Wagnac, to act as interpreter and meet again the next day.

The following day, Rose, Miquette and John met at Carmel's house. The atmosphere there was strange, dark and cool, almost like Carmel was a fortune teller. The conversation was very emotional with John thanking Rose for Farah and Cherline and Rose thanking John for taking them and giving them a life. Nothing was discussed about Miquette at the time, although John met with Miquette another day at Gladys Sylvestre's house, some 8-10 blocks away from the guest house.

Later, John went to Rose's house to meet Rose's family. He remembers the family as being gracious and friendly, and remembers the house as being a one room concrete block dwelling with

19

a blue door. The cooking was done on the outside. There was also an outhouse outside. John was told somebody always stayed home so it wouldn't be robbed.

Don't Break A Poor Haitian Girl's Heart

In discussions with Gladys Sylvestre, John raised the subject of the possibility of Miquette coming to America to study and finish her education. Gladys was enthused about the idea, but advised caution in broaching the subject. "Don't break a poor Haitian girl's heart," she warned, "This will be very difficult to accomplish, so if you don't intend to see it through, don't even start."

Later, with another woman acting as interpreter, John asked Miquette if she would be interested in coming to the U.S. As the interpreter translated his question, Miquette started squealing and jumping up and down in glee. The interpreter, a French woman staying at the guest house, said to John "Do you really need my interpretation of her answer?" Miquette was thrilled, of course, to consider the opportunity, but afraid it might be impossible.

John advised Miquette to spend the next year studying English, obtaining a passport and making necessary connections to secure an endorsement from a Haitian Rotary Club. Meanwhile, John promised he would return to his Rotary Club in Detroit Lakes to challenge them to sponsor Miquette as an exchange student. Normally, a host club would provide three homes for a visiting foreign student with each of three families providing a home for 1/3 of the year. But in this case, the Lee family volunteered to take Miquette for the full year. Detroit Lakes Rotary president, Bob Harris, now deceased, worked very hard to prepare the way for the Detroit Lakes Noon Rotary Club to sponsor Miquette.

Miquette's family was most enthused about this dream arrangement. Miquette's proud older brother, Pidens (they call him "Dens") offered John even more encouragement: "My sister Miquette is verrry intelligent" he bragged.

A memorable moment for John in Haiti is when he went to church with Rose and Beatrice on Mother's Day. Rose sat on one side of him and Beatrice on the other. He could see the faces of Farah and Cherline in their faces. "Mary and I are so blessed to have the daughters of these mothers" he thought. John left Haiti in hopes that Miquette would be able to come to Detroit Lakes in 2000.

But when he left, Miquette had problems connecting with the Rotary Club in Port au Prince. Their attitude seemed to be "why should we sponsor this poor girl?" She definitely was not of the class they would normally endorse. But, Gladys Sylvestre connected Miquette with Dr. Claude Surena, a Rotary Club member, who took Miquette to Rotary meetings and persuaded the club to play ball. Dr. Surena also assisted Miquette with her exchange paper work. Meanwhile, Miquette was diligently studying English and had obtained a passport from Haitian authorities.

But, getting a visa from the U.S. authorities to visit America was a much more difficult matter. This would require an interview with Miquette and they wouldn't grant one. The summer of 2000 had arrived and the clock was ticking. With the end of July approaching and school starting in a month, Lee decided he would have to fly to Haiti again to try to push the visa through. He contacted an American dentist he had met in Haiti the previous summer. The dentist was going on another mission trip and arranged space for Lee on a DC-3 cargo plane for a flight to Port au Prince and space for Lee and Miquette (based on Lee's determination, hope and faith) for a flight back.

Give Me Your Tired, Your Poor

The path in Port au Prince was cluttered with obstructions. In the first place, Lee had to pay a fee to the U.S. government to get an appointment for a Visa interview. Then he and Miquette were directed to an alley outside the U.S. Consulate to wait to be called. There were "hustlers" in line offering to sell places nearer the front of the line. Most discouraging. Besides, Lee learned he would not be allowed to be with Miquette for the interview. More frustration. Miquette was finally called in for her interview. Five minutes later, she was back out in the alley. The interviewing officer had asked her one question: "What's up?" Not understanding his idiom, Miquette looked skyward. Her application for a Visa was denied. Lee couldn't believe it. Every document was in order, but still she had been denied.

Lee took Miquette and went to a different part of the consulate and was able to ask a question of an official through a bulletproof window. He was told no request for a second appointment could be made in person—it must be made by phone. He had to walk about two blocks to find a phone to call back to the consulate. He was given the impression that the U.S. would be most reluctant to allow this poor, young Haitian to come to America because she would just want to stay and would become a "ward" of our country without any means of support. Lee was

22

told he could get an appointment in a week. He then asked for an appointment with two other officers under the Consul General. He was told that appointments could not be made by telephone but must be requested by U.S. mail.

He was totally disgusted and embarrassed to be an American. He contrasted the hard attitude he was being shown by U.S. officials with the inscription on our Statue of Liberty, written by Emma Lazarus:

> Give me your tired, your poor,
> Your huddled masses yearning to breathe free,
> The wretched refuse of your teeming shore,
> Send these, the homeless, tempest tossed,
> I lift my lamp beside the golden door.

I Feel Like A Good Cry

He emailed his wife, Mary, back at home. He said "I am very discouraged at the moment . . . I hope I do not have to come home alone. I feel like a good cry." Lee, expecting more delay, composed a letter to the Consul General, pleading for understanding and help. Here are portions of the letter:

Mr. Roger Daily, Consul General of the United States
104, Rue Oswald Durand
Port au Prince, Haiti

Dear Mr. Daily,

My name is John Lee. I am a Lutheran pastor and member of the Detroit Lakes Rotary Club. This club, in cooperation with a Rotary Club in Port au Prince, has chosen Miquette Denie of Port au Prince as a Youth Exchange Student. Our club is sponsoring two students this year. The other student is a young man from Japan who just arrived in Detroit Lakes. I came to Haiti on behalf of the Rotary Club to escort Ms. Denie to Minnesota.

I accompanied her to your office this morning and waited in the alley behind the Consular section for her to secure a visa. I was most surprised to have her explain to me, after her interview, that she was denied a visa because she did not have enough money and she was not fluent in English. When I sought confirmation of this report from the guard at the back gate, I was sent upstairs to inquire.

The man upstairs was good enough to go downstairs and he returned with the same report that Miquette had given me, that due to lack of money and language skills she was not given a visa. I told him there had to be a misunderstanding that she was under full scholarship, which included a monthly allowance for personal needs, (this information in the IAP-66). I also explained that our students require minimal English skills. We have a special "ESL-English as a Second Language" program in the Detroit Lakes school system and both students will be enrolled in it as necessary. (I must also add that I speak neither Creole nor French and she has been translating for me.) At any rate, the man behind the window could not help me with the particulars. He did give me the phone numbers to make an appointment with Consular Officer.

I left the office and called from a pay phone. I eventually talked to a man who would not identify himself. (I later learned he was the man who interviewed Ms. Denie.) He informed me that the decision made was final and I could appeal it in six months. When I explained that our program was starting soon and asked him for any other possible options, he said I could write to you and request an appointment with you.

I returned to the upstairs office to confirm your name and address. There Ms. Denie saw her interviewer standing in a back office, and I was informed that the man I had talked to on the phone was this same interviewer. I was unable to talk to him or to learn his name, (due to privacy rights), and I was also told that Ms. Denie did not have the right to know his name either. By this time I was very tired and I requested that I be able to simply sit down and talk with another human being without having to stand in front of a glass window, but that request was not even acknowledged. Dear Sir, as a minister I am not used to treating people in this way or to being treated with such poor regard. Perhaps I was not as patient as I could have been. I do know I was very disappointed and discouraged as I waited and walked from place to place and person to person. I do not believe I have, but if my persistence offended anyone in your office, I apologize.

I am now requesting your help. One man in your office made a decision not to grant this visa. Two hundred Rotarians, seven hundred church members, the staff of the Detroit Lakes High School, and US Congressman Collin Peterson have all made their decision and expressed their desire to have Ms. Denie as an exchange student. We are very proud of our exchange program. It has been a great benefit to many students and to the Detroit Lakes community. Please grant Ms. Denie a J-1 visa so that she can join our community for one year.

I am able to stay in Port au Prince for one more week. I was hoping to leave on Tuesday, September 5, but I can delay travel plans until Thursday noon, September 7. I assumed the IAP-66 form was proof of financial backing, but I enclose additional documents showing that her airline ticket is being paid by my congregation, Bakke Lutheran Church.

I request an appointment with you on Friday, September 1 or Tuesday, September 5. The Guest House where I am staying does not have an operating telephone, but I can be reached through the pastor of Quisqueya Chapel, Karl Olson, at 401-3667 or through Ms. Gladys Sylvestre, and Hope Hospital, 246-1944 or 246-2721, or at her personal phone, 401-1781.

Thank you for considering this request.

The letter was not sent, as the pastor and his wife decided to call on a higher power. Mary called the Office of Congressman Collin Peterson in Detroit Lakes and spoke with his administrative assistant, Sharon Josephson. Josephson immediately called the Office of the Consul General in Port au Prince. When she related the problem, she was told the Consul General would call her back. "No, I'm staying on the line until you give me the Consul General." Finally, she got through and demanded an appointment for John and Miquette the next day. Since a Congressman's office was calling, the interview was granted.

John was challenged by the Consul General, Mr. Daily. "How will we know this girl will ever return to Haiti?" John said, "I will personally bring her back a year from now." "I will hold you personally responsible," Daily told him. Little did John know that his promise to Mr. Daily could play a big role in Miquette's future.

Miquette got her visa on the spot. John and Miquette gathered her things and rushed to catch the DC-3—Miquette's first plane ride. The 1937 vintage plane was uninsulated, drafty, chilly and got colder as the altitude increased. Skinny Miquette was shivering and hugging herself to stay warm.

The plane landed in Miami where John and Miquette saw an American flag flying. John stood at attention, saluted, and made this declaration to Miquette: "On behalf of the government of the United States of America, I want to welcome you to our country. We are glad you're here!" Miquette laughed.

Miquette was jolted even before she arrived in Minnesota. In Florida she heard her first broadcast in English, and, although she had studied some English, she couldn't understand a word of it. The language was her biggest challenge. To start with, she translated everything she read to Creole or French in order to understand it.

When they landed in Minneapolis, they immediately hit the highway for the 200 mile trip to the Lee home in Detroit Lakes. They stopped for a break and a sandwich at St. Cloud. Two women in the restaurant stared at Miquette and John overheard one comment: "That's disgusting." John thought he was hearing a racial slur, but, seconds later he heard "She's so skinny." And she was. She weighed about 105 pounds and her arms and legs were bones.

The initial walk through the front door of the Lee home in Detroit Lakes was tense. Farah and Cherline were upstairs whispering. They were shy and scared. They hadn't seen Miquette for 11 years and she was a stranger to them. Miquette remembered the girls only as tots. She was excited to see them, but scared too. It was a memorable moment for all three, and poignant too for Mary Lee, who had never met Miquette before. Miquette had just turned 20, but she spoke very little English, so her arrival was awkward for Miquette, the girls and the Lees.

CHAPTER 4

STARTING FROM SCRATCH

*"My music had roots which I dug up from
my own childhood, musical roots buried
in the darkest soil."*

—*Ray Charles*

At this point we should go back to get acquainted with Miquette Denie, her childhood and her stop-and-go education.

Miquette was born (as she now knows) on June 8th, 1980, the sixth of nine children, in St. Michel, a town about 150 miles north of Port au Prince in the Central Plateau region. The first child Wilfrid, died at the age of one. Next came Beatrice (the mother of Cherline), Sandra, Pidens (known now as "Dens"), Kateline (who died in 1993 at the age of 15 of hallucinations with a high fever, no exact cause of death recorded), then Miquette, Isaac (just finished medical school—Miquette helped with his high school expenses and John and Mary Lee made all his medical school payments), Farah and the youngest, Camisha ("Misha"), about 22 in 2013, who was adopted by a Canadian family when she was less than a week old. Miquette saw Misha at birth, then in 2006 in Detroit Lakes and in Haiti in 2012. Misha, whom Miquette calls a "free spirit," now lives in Vancouver in British Columbia.

Miquette started school at the age of four at the Nazarene church school at a cost of $10 per year, payable in quarterly installments, yet her family struggled to make the payments. Her dad, Cleuis, was a free-lance carpenter who had jobs when he was called. He had never been to school, never learned to read or write and had never held a pen. Mom, Rose, couldn't read or write either. She signed her name with an X. Rose held three jobs. She was a maid in a private home where she worked, cleaned and did laundry. She also did laundry and cleaning at a hospital. Finally, she did cooking at Miquette's school where the food program was operated by a missionary. Her wages for all three jobs came to less than $50 per month. Miquette went to school every year, but no year was complete. The school years were divided into trimesters. If a student's fees weren't paid before a trimester exam the student was sent home and couldn't take the required exams. Class work didn't count—only the trimester exam. Miquette missed many exams for lack of funds. (The Haitian currency, by the way, was not the dollar, but the gourde. One dollar was approximately 40 gourdes.)

Miquette's school had no classrooms and no privacy. Grades 1 and 2 were clustered together as were grades 3 and 4 as well as 5 and 6. The teaching was riddled with interruptions and distractions.

In St. Michel, Cleuis was working but he left home early and came home late. Dens was in and out of school, mostly working with his dad as a carpenter, and wasn't able to be of much help at home. Kateline, the sister who died at 15, was leading the family. Miquette, age 10, was taking care of the house, shopping for groceries, cooking, doing her homework, and making sure Isaac was doing his.

Education was more important to Rose than to Cleuis. Cleuis wanted as much help as possible from Dens in his carpentry work. Cleuis turned most of his earnings over to Rose for management. Rose's attitude was that you should get two meals a day, but from time to time, we'll eat only once so we can pay for school. Sometimes the family was hungry.

In the summer when school was out, Miquette visited her mother in Port au Prince. She traveled alone by taxi (tap-tap) to Gonaives, a significant city where the documents of Haitian independence were signed, and from Gonaives by bus to Port au Prince. The year she was 12, she was returning to St. Michel and she got off the bus to catch a tap-tap to St. Michel. She had money in her pocket from her mother for school fees and tap-tap fare. She was in a crowd and could feel somebody touching her. She felt in her pocket and the money was gone. A big guy was running away so she chased him, screaming "He took my money."

People discouraged her from chasing the guy – "Leave him alone—it's not safe. People get killed." But he had her money and she was determined to get it back. She chased him for about 10 minutes until he cut through a back yard and went into a house. Several men were playing cards and dominos outside the house. She screamed at the guy in the house, "You took my money and I'm not leaving until I get it back." He taunted her "Why don't you come in and get it?" She refused but didn't leave. One of the men playing cards said "You are a brave girl." Then he went into the house and took the money from the thief and returned it to Miquette. Both Rose and Cleuis scolded her, telling her she could have been killed. But the driven Miquette learned another lesson—determination pays off—this is how to survive.

Miquette and her siblings had an uncle in St. Michel, their mother's younger brother, Tayan. Tayan was a skilled cabinet maker who also made furniture and coffins and he was successful. Tayan and his wife had three children, two girls and a boy, close in age to Miquette and her family. Tayan's children always had nice clothes, were very clean and were very nice to their cousins. But they had better food, three meals a day and were taken care of in ways Cleuis and Rose couldn't care for their children. Tayan's wife worked and smelled great. The Denies loved their uncle and cousins, but they were envious. Sometimes they wished the aunt and uncle were their parents.

Uncle Tayon had a big, long bike that would carry one kid in front and two behind on a rack. He rode his kids to school every day. Sometimes the admiring Miquette and her brother Dens, imitating their uncle, would go downtown in St. Michel, rent a bike for 5¢ (about two gourde) and ride together.

The cousins considered their uncle Tayon about the richest man in St. Michel. After all, his family had the only TV in the neighborhood. The kids in the neighborhood (as many as 20 at a time) would hang around outside Tayan's house and look at the TV through the windows—especially when Haitian soccer was on the screen.

Uncle Tayan was kind and generous to his nieces and nephews. He looked out for their welfare and provided some financial assistance. Tayan died in January, 2014. His family still lives in St. Michel today.

Sometimes when tuition money was short and Miquette was worried about missing a trimester she would buy vegetables like mangos or avocados then resell them door to door. This was a convenience for the homeowners, so there was some business to be had. Sometimes mangos just fall off trees, so Miquette just gathered the "windfall," peddled them and hopefully in a week or so there would be enough money to return to school. As Miquette got older, the tuition cost had risen to $20-$25 for the year.

Both in St. Michel and later in Port au Prince, Miquette was very involved in the church (she called church her "refuge") and in Girl Scouts. In the Girl Scout program there were regular breakfasts, dancing and classes. She was taught about teen pregnancy, a serious problem in Haiti, and was lectured to "protect yourself."

May 18th is Flag Day in Haiti—a day for parades, uniforms and dancing in the street. Children practiced all year for the parade. The Girl Scout uniform was all white—white jacket, white pants, white hat—like a military uniform. Miquette's dad borrowed $20 so she could have a uniform. The children, waving colorful ribbons, parade through the streets all through St. Michel. There were big crowds of cheering people and the event was very exciting for Miquette.

Since Miquette's mom was in Port au Prince and her dad was busy with his carpentry work in St. Michel, the church and Girl Scout activities kept her out of trouble. When she was smaller, she had fun (even though they had no toys)—jumping rope, playing hide and seek and other kids' games. At night when there was a full moon, children would assemble, sit in a circle, and tell stories and riddles.

As she got older, many kids were just hanging out in the streets and getting into trouble. Teen pregnancy was common. Miquette decided early to avoid that scene. But one of her close friends was part of it. She came and went as the mood moved her and her parents didn't care. Miquette watched but chose Girl Scouts instead. Besides, she said, boys were afraid of her dad—big hands, big fists and a fierce look—he scared some away. Her best friend from first grade, Anouse, had the same values as Miquette. They are still best friends. Miquette visits her whenever she is in St. Michel. Anouse has three children and struggles now, but the friendship is solid.

Miquette's Nazarene Church School in St. Michel had a rule. If you go to our school you will attend church every Sunday. They took roll. There were no absences without a good reason. For Miquette it was good—lessons were learned.

Miquette remembers that Mother's Day was a day of celebration in Haiti: a day of songs, dances and poems. She recalls being in a group of 10 children performing – singing, and dancing. She stepped forward with a poem about her mother then stepped back to finish with the group.

Looking back at her years in St. Michel, Miquette had one regret—no pictures. No baby pictures, no school pictures, no pictures in her Girl Scout uniform and no family pictures.

Miquette and Cleuis moved to Port au Prince to join Rose, Dens and Isaac when Miquette was 15. Rose came to get them in a tap-tap that arrived and honked for them at 4:00 a.m. The tap-tap pickup carried 15-20 people. Miquette's luggage was one bag the size of a big purse. They rode to Gonaives and caught a bus from there. The bus was a school bus. Miquette was beginning to feel like a city girl because there were cars in Gonaives, but very few in St. Michel.

When they arrived in Port au Prince, Miquette was thrilled—the people, the traffic, the sounds—it all seemed very exciting. This was a city. They even had electricity almost full time. But initially she was frightened by the police and their guns—the guns always seemed to be pointed at someone.

What she remembers most fondly was the reunion of her entire family. They were together again for the first time in 5 years. But her mother's job at the orphanage required her to live there. Thursday was Rose's day off so that was a special family day.

Miquette was excited about her new school too, although it was small and stark with benches instead of desks, unpainted, unfinished and unclean. She had a great teacher and is still in touch with him to this very day. His name is Osma, an older man, a father figure. He was kind, compassionate and really loved his students. He told Miquette she would always do well. When she was in the 6th grade, her big brother Dens was in the 7th grade in the same school and they went to school together. He was looking out for her but struggling academically.

Before students in Haiti can advance from the 6th grade to the 7th, a major national exam called Certificat, lasting two days, must be taken and passed. In preparation, Miquette and her classmates had group studies on weekends. Miquette tutored her friends. It is traditional for the children to "dress up" in their very best for the exam with a different outfit each day. Miquette didn't have three outfits, but her older sister Sandra washed, ironed and put old outfits together to look clean and new. They may have been poor but they didn't want to look poor. The exam results were posted on the school walls at the end of July. Miquette passed.

Miquette went to a bigger school for the 7th grade. The cost was higher: $50 admission fee plus $8 per month. Students were not allowed to begin the year until the admission fee was paid. There were two sessions each day and Miquette went to the afternoon session because it was slightly cheaper. Rose had a steady income from her job at the orphanage, but Cleuis' income was sporadic, so it was essentially up to Rose to come up with the monthly fees, but she couldn't always do it. And, in Port au Prince there were no mangos or avocados for Miquette to pick up and sell, and she was unable to attend some months. So, starting in the 7th grade, Miquette began picking up part-time jobs to help pay for school. One job was working as a substitute nanny for children with special needs. She also did some washing, mopping and laundry. At the orphanage when Rose washed, one of the nuns went to the convent on weekends and paid Miquette to take care of some of her duties. Miquette turned the money over to her mother to manage.

This is how the 7th and 8th grade went for Miquette—mostly school, homework, part-time jobs, Sunday School teacher, youth leader, not much time for horsing around or getting into trouble.

Seventh grade studies required double the number of books, adding to the already imposing expense. Miquette worked out an arrangement with several other students for joint ownership of books. They stayed after school, exchanged notes and borrowed, traded and shared the books the best they could.

In the 8th grade, Miquette's part-time job opportunities were diminished because orphanage employees weren't taking as much time off. Now what? Rose had a good friend named Carmel Wagnac who was kind, well to do and generous. She sent her children to good schools and even traveled to the United States. Carmel helped Rose pay Miquette's school fees that year. Miquette didn't miss much school in the 8th grade because Carmel came to the rescue when the squeeze was on. Miquette loved visiting Carmel at her home because of Carmel's obvious affection for her. It made the visits all the more sweet because she usually got food there. Carmel gave Miquette a very nice dress for her 16th birthday—her first birthday present ever. Carmel now lives in Chicago.

Miquette's best friend from the 7th through the 9th grade was Beatrice (not her sister, Beatrice) who is still her friend today. They were the same size, including their big size 10 feet, so they loaned clothes to one another. Miquette would wear an outfit one week, Beatrice would wear something else and the following week they'd reverse the order. Miquette and Beatrice would walk past a sidewalk café and say "look at all the rich people eating in there."

At the end of the 8th grade came another end-of-the-year test. If you didn't pass it, you had to repeat the entire last grade before you could move up. Again, Miquette passed.

In the 9th grade Miquette was one of the top three students in her class, including her friend Beatrice and a boy named Wilson. She loved her English class. The teacher was one who would either make you love or hate the class. It was taught with such passion that Miquette loved it. The students were required to take their tests in isolation so nobody would cheat. On Saturdays, Miquette helped tutor a study group in physics and chemistry—at no pay.

Flag Day, May 18th, was a big day in Port au Prince as it had been in St. Michel. The school rented a bus, packed kids with their food from home and drove to the beach. It was a day of color and at this age, uniforms were not worn. Instead, everybody dressed their best. Miquette didn't appreciate the holiday—she had one pair of shoes and didn't have the clothes to match the festive mood. About once a month was a day of color, including Valentine's Day, and Miquette dreaded every one.

Miquette finished the 9th grade at the age of 18. In the 10th grade she studied Latin, Spanish, English, Haitian Creole and French. When she was 19, Haiti had a 13 year educational program, so if she had remained in her home country she would have been 22 when she finished high school.

CHAPTER 5

WELCOME TO DETROIT LAKES— YOU'RE A LAKER NOW

"There are a million rules for being a girl.
There are a million things you have to do
to get through each day. High School has things
that can trip you up, ruin you.
People say one thing and mean another,
and you have to know all the rules,
you have to know what you can and can't do."

—*Elizabeth Scott, the Unwritten Rules*

When John and Miquette arrived at the Lee home, Miquette commented that there were no walls around the house and no gate. Nice homes in Haiti were necessarily walled and gated. This was only the beginning of her culture shock in America.

School had already started and Miquette was several days late. John took Miquette to school the next day and went with her to every class. Miquette entered school as a twenty year old junior. Mary went with Miquette the next day to several classes as well. Miquette was overwhelmed. She recognized some of the English, but the teachers and everybody were talking way too fast. Farah was in the 9th grade and she was embarrassed by her sister's presence, especially when the other kids heard Miquette's age. Every night there was tutoring at the kitchen table. Miquette worked hard—she was motivated and determined, but she was still overwhelmed.

Coming to Minnesota, Miquette told herself "Life is hard in Haiti—my year in Detroit Lakes will be a breeze." But it wasn't. She had to keep telling herself "My purpose here is to get an education, something to take back to Haiti. Stick with it and you will be a better person when you return." Gradually, conversation was becoming easier for her and she was understanding her homework.

What a wonderful surprise she had in her first week of classes when in Gail Kotschevar's history class, Ms. Kotschevar announced "Go grab your book and write your name in the book." Miquette approached her. "How do I get a book? I have no money." The teacher told her the books were free—just return them at the end of the year. What a thrill. Miquette had never had the money to get books in Haiti. The practice there was for classmates to share, trade and pass books around. Ms. Kotschevar later commented that Miquette demonstrated "a strong work ethic and a keen desire to excel in school. As an example, at the beginning of the school year Miquette had no experience with the computer, by the end of the year, she was able to do power point presentations."

One very bright spot in school for Miquette was her biology class. Her teacher, Vicki Welke, was very patient and understanding. She spent time with the frightened student, tutored her after class, and sent books home with her to help her through the challenges of language, loneliness and a scary, foreign environment.

Geometry was a special problem. Miquette had never had toys so she had no idea what square or triangle meant. She had never handled objects with known shapes. She never had crayons as a child and had never drawn anything. Geometry was hugely challenging for her. Keyboarding was also a serious problem for Miquette. She had never seen a computer before and didn't even know how to turn one on. To start with, Miquette took notes in French, translating from what English she could understand. Everybody continued to talk too fast.

Oh My Gosh, You Were In The Boys Bathroom

Miquette felt awkward among her high school classmates. First of all, she was known to be 20 years old and some made fun of her age. Also, she was tall and skinny—she says a size 0 was baggy on her. In Haiti, school bathrooms were unisex. One day in her first week at Detroit Lakes High School, Miquette went into a bathroom without knowing it was different here. When she told her sister, Farah, about the puzzling situation, Farah said "Oh, my gosh, you were in the boys bathroom."

It got worse. In health class each girl received a "care" package of health products. Miquette opened her package in a school bus surrounded by fellow students, boys and girls. One by one she removed the products, then expressed curiosity about an item she had never seen before. She pulled out a tampon, sniffed it and started picking away the layers. "What is this?" she asked. She heard only silence in response as the students just watched and rolled their eyes. More embarrassment. Farah was mortified when she heard the story.

The school environment was not welcoming to Miquette. The girls were territorial and the boys were intimidated. Miquette was amazed at how many of her classmates had little or no regard for this gift of education. She was astonished that students would cut classes out of boredom or indifference.

She said that the Lees were "the glue that held me together" in the early months. They felt like parents to her. One or the other would stay up as late as midnight with her helping her with her homework. Then the next morning there was always breakfast on the table by 6:30.

Miquette received two allowances—one from the Lees and the other from Rotary. During her first year she was spending very little, hiding surplus money under her mattress and sending what she could back to her family in Haiti. She did not tell the Lees about this of course.

American Christmas customs were amazing to Miquette. She was overwhelmed by her first Christmas in America. She couldn't believe the tree, the decorations, the food, the gifts, the parties and the reunions. The Lee family has a tradition of serving oyster stew for their Christmas eve meal—she loved it. Her Christmas experience in Haiti had been almost zero. When she returned to her homeland, she made sure that the children in TeacHaiti schools experienced parties, Santa Claus and gifts.

She had nightmares often that first year. She woke up screaming and frightened. Some of the dreams were about snakes in Haiti. Sometimes she screamed and scratched the walls. She was not accustomed to such a soft bed, so she occasionally slept on the floor.

She was lonely that first year. She missed her family and friends in Haiti. Even her sisters, Farah and Cherline, now the Lee girls, were strangers to her and she was a stranger to them. They didn't feel like family to her until the entire Lee family went to Haiti together at the end of that first year. About the only school friend she had early that first year was a Japanese girl named Ai Jin, another foreign student also struggling to learn English. She received a letter from Haiti telling her one of her good friends had died. She cried and cried, devastated that she couldn't go back to be there at such a sad time. One detour from loneliness was provided by Rotary. Twice during the year, Rotary sponsored a gathering of international exchange students. One was in Duluth and one was at the Maplelag Center near Detroit Lakes. The students comforted one another by sharing their mutual experiences and puzzlements.

My Face Hurts

The skinny Haitian couldn't believe how cold the winters were in Minnesota. One day, walking to school with John Lee, she said, "My face hurts." But more amazing to her than the pain of a winter wind was expressed in a letter she wrote to Haiti telling about walking on the frozen water.

American food was strange to Miquette, but she never complained. She had grown up on rice, beans and chicken sauce. She was shown the groceries in the cupboards and refrigerator. "This is for us." Miquette had never seen so much food in her life. She told Mary much later that sometimes she would come down to look in the refrigerator while everybody was sleeping to see if the food was still there. Her home in Haiti had no electricity, so certainly no refrigerator. The idea of eating leftovers was new to her. First of all, there had never been more than enough. Secondly, without refrigerators, the food would spoil—it could kill you.

Miquette did some cooking for the family. When she did, she cooked what was the first choice for her and her sisters—rice, beans and chicken sauce. It reminded them of their meals at home in Haiti. She was a good cook and the family enjoyed her meals. One of her specialties was "soup joumou," squash soup, a traditional Haitian soup from the days of the slave rebellion in 1800. But Miquette was not familiar with American spices. To determine the flavor of these powders and seeds, she explored her way through the tins, jars and little bottles of the spice cabinet sniffing and tasting.

As the year went on, Farah and Cherline gradually warmed up to their older sister (technically, sister and aunt, but they will both be referred to as sisters in this book). But other friends were few. Because she was concentrating on academics, she was not active in extra-curricular activities, although she loved to sing and enjoyed being in Kathy Larson's choir. She was athletic and a natural runner and started to go out for track, but when the dots were connected, Miquette's 20 years made her ineligible so that was the end of track. Her sister Farah, was a great sprinter on the team that year while Cherline specialized in the pole vault.

Probably her top activity of the school year was youth programs at the Bakke Lutheran Church, one of John Lee's rural churches, where she developed more friendships and continued to improve her English skills.

Carl Lee was 19 years old during the year Miquette spent with the family. He is a fast talker. Forward to the end of the year when Miquette could understand just about everything Carl was saying, she knew she'd turned the corner with the English language. By the end of the school year, her studies were getting easier for her—after hours and hours of homework. She studied harder than her classmates. She was getting mostly A's and B's in her classes and was beginning to realize her potential even though she still couldn't speak fluently.

Exchange students, under the terms of their visa, are not permitted to be employed for wages. So the summer of 2001 consisted of camps and educational opportunities for Miquette. She spent June 11-15 at a French Concordia Language Village near Bemidji, then later at a family Haiti camp at Alexandria where she was able to visit again with Gladys Sylvestre, the Director of the Foundation for children of Haiti who came every summer from Haiti to stay in touch with Haitian children and their American families.

Miquette's one-year visa was fast running out and she would soon return to Haiti. She wanted very much to continue going to school in the U.S., but the limited visa and finances were hurdles. If she continued as a student at Detroit Lakes High School, her status as a foreign exchange student would be lost and the cost of non-resident tuition would be an unreachable $13,000. There was a discussion among the Lees about sponsoring Miquette for one year of school at the private Quisqueya School in Port au Prince, which was encouragement for Miquette. That would have been Plan B.

In July, John Lee learned of the possibility of Miquette attending Oak Grove Lutheran High School in Fargo, ND for her senior year at a lower tuition. The president of Oak Grove, John Andreason, was a former pastor in the Detroit Lakes area and an acquaintance of John's. John and Miquette traveled to Fargo for an interview with Andreason. Would Oak Grove accept Miquette? Yes, but the tuition would be $8,000.

How to raise the $8,000? Time was short. There was a Rotary meeting on Thursday of that week and the family was scheduled to take Miquette back to Haiti the following week on August 8th. On July 29th, when it was still thought that Miquette would be returning to Haiti, the Bakke Church organized a potluck fundraiser for Miquette. The Lees provided the traditional Creole enrtre' of avec poule riz et pois.

Then John went to his Noon Rotary Club to plead for funds. By that time, the Rotarians knew Miquette. They knew that she looked them in the eye when she shook their hands and somehow had natural social graces. And she had charm—it was showing through. John was given only a few minutes to state his case. "You all know Miquette," he said "She's scheduled to return to Haiti next week. We can't afford the $13,000 tuition it would take to keep her in Detroit Lakes High School, but she can go to Oak Grove for $8,000. We can keep her here, but we need your help. "Before the meeting was over, $4,000 had been pledged. John's Dad volunteered $1,000 and John and Mary came up with $2,000 while the other $1,000 came in nickels and dimes, bits and pieces. The goal was met.

But the battle wasn't won. Before Miquette could go to Oak Grove, she would need a long-term Visa.

CHAPTER 6

FAMILY REUNION IN HAITI

"The family is more sacred than the state."

—Pope Pius XI

It was planned that John and Mary Lee would make the trip to Haiti with Miquette, Farah and Cherline. Farah and Cherline had not seen their mother, father and Haitian family since 12 years earlier, in June 1989. After tickets for the five had been purchased, Cherline asked a good question: "Why aren't Dan and Carl coming? They should experience Haiti too—this is important to me." After all, Dan and Carl were her brothers. So the Lees scrambled to get tickets for the boys too. The flight was booked on a DC-3. "Missionary flights" were flown on DC-3 for folks who had "missions" in Haiti. They were cheaper than standard commercial flying, but were bare-bones as far as comfort is concerned. More cumbersome, but more cargo and supplies were allowed.

When the family arrived at the airport at Port au Prince, Rose was there with her son, Pidens, and daughter, Beatrice. The scene was chaotic. Rose and Beatrice were hugging their daughters and Miquette was acting as interpreter. Cherline and Farah had forgotten their Haitian Creole and nobody else was on hand to facilitate communications. The parties moved through the terminal, then outdoors in the parking and taxi area. The heat and humidity in August are brutal. The main objective of the trip to Haiti was to secure a new visa for Miquette so she could return to school in the

United States. Only one car was available (two had been planned, but one didn't arrive) to take the family and visitors into the city, so almost immediately that car, driven by Miquette's brother Dens, rushed away with John and Miquette to buy an appointment for a visa application and interview. "We'll be back," they said.

Mary and her four children were left standing there sweating in the sun while taxi drivers were tugging at their luggage to gain a fare. Miquette and John were gone while the families stood there waiting, unable to carry on a conversation. About all they could do is to make a few awkward gestures and smile at one another. Mary, hanging on to her kids and the luggage, was scared. Rose and Beatrice, poor women, trying to make the visitors comfortable, brought treats for the children.

John and Miquette went to a bank to pay for the visa appointment. Miquette would not be allowed to return to the U.S. a second time as an exchange student. This time she would be required to seek a longer term visa. They learned bad news. The rules had changed—there was a required two week waiting period before a visa could be granted. But the Lees had already purchased seven return tickets for seven days later.

The Lees were determined they would not leave Miquette in Haiti. They had already raised the necessary money for her room, board and tuition at Oak Grove. Would John have to stay with her and fight it out with the authorities—again?

Finally, almost two hours later, John, Miquette and Dens returned and rescued the families. They all piled into the car together and drove into the city. But John and Miquette were worried about getting another visa under the new rules.

As the families were driving into the Port au Prince from the airport, Carl was sitting at an open window with his elbow out trying to get cool. Dens, who knew some English, told him he had better get his arm in the car. "Why?" asked Carl. "Dangerous," was the answer. Carl pulled his arm in and only seconds later the mirror from another car banged the side of Den's car where Carl's elbow had been.

While they were driving they noticed a worker welding rebar with a wire connected to an overhead power line. The welding rod was being held by a wooden stick. The electric arc was visible. The welder was wearing only sunglasses for eye protection, turning his head and looking out of the corner of his eye. Carl was startled—"Look at that!"

The Lee family was delivered to the Guest House. This house is operated by the Foundation for the Children of Haiti. It had surrounding walls and gate, electricity (sometimes) and running water. The Foundation also ran the Hope Hospital, a handicap home, a school and an orphanage (they call it a nursery). The orphanage is not a permanent home for the children, but a temporary placement center for children waiting to be adopted by families in the United States, Canada and France. The chief officer of these enterprises was Gladys Sylvestre, now Gladys Sylvestre Thomas, the same person who came to the Haiti Camps in America.

John Lee called the U.S. consulate to attempt to change the visa appointment from two weeks to a day within his seven day ticket window. One year before he had promised he would personally deliver Miquette back. The secretary John talked to made him an appointment to see the Consul General himself, not just an immigration officer, in just 40 minutes.

Gladys Sylvestre Thomas provided a driver to hustle John, Miquette and Mary Lee to the consulate. The driver was driving a tiny van and he arrived late—very late, with 20 minutes of the allotted interview time of 45 minutes already gone. The four squeezed into the van and hung on for the ride of their lives through Port au Prince traffic. It was like a movie chase scene: full speed, middle of the street, on the sidewalk, horn honking, coming within inches of vehicles and pedestrians. Mary was nearly hysterical. "John, (in the front seat with the driver) tell him to slow down. I don't want to die in this country." Miquette wasn't concerned. When they arrived at the consulate, they had to wait briefly for the appointment. They weren't late at all.

Before the appointment, Mary advised the very emotional and excitable Miquette that if the Consul General granted the visa "Don't jump up and down and go wild—don't hug and kiss the guy. Wait with any demonstration until we get outside." They hoped to impress the Consul General; they brought report cards and pictures, memories of Rotary activities—an entire presentation. The official was very gracious. He read all the materials. He asked Miquette questions about what she had done in America for the past year. This was the report John Lee had promised to make a year earlier. When they told him they wanted to extend the visa and take her back to the U.S., the Consul General was not happy to hear the request. This was not the deal. They told him she wanted to become a nurse and would need to return for nursing studies. The Consul General said "You told me one year." They were asking for five more years to finish high school and get a college degree.

John replied that the best place to get a nursing education was in the U.S. "We have secured financial support through churches, Rotary and individuals. She has been accepted at Oak Grove. None of this could happen in Haiti." Throughout this interview, Miquette was speaking too—in English.

Then the Consul General asked whether Miquette would get a job back in

Haiti. They said yes, Gladys Sylvestre Thomas will hire her at the hospital. The Consul General said, "Who is this Gladys you say will hire her? I need to meet her."

So, arrangements were made for a second interview a day or two later. Gladys agreed to come. She even provided a driver again—this time the driver was on time. John, Mary, Miquette and Gladys appeared for the second interview. Everything was riding on this one.

Gladys was a powerhouse as she made a clear declarative statement: "I will hire her when she returns." But the Consul General was not prepared to give in easily. He said, "I can't issue a new visa that quickly." Little Gladys, speaking softly, but looking him straight in the eye, said "Yes you can." He said, "We'll have to schedule another appointment." Again, Gladys looked at him and said softly, "No you won't."

The General surrendered. He granted the visa and it was printed that very day. But he added some advice. He said, "You don't need a visa to stay in the U.S., only to get in. Don't come back to Haiti until you have your degree. If you do, you will never get back. I will be retiring and I won't be here to help."

What if Gladys hadn't been there for this showdown with the Counsel General? John would have had to stay in Haiti with Miquette until they could have further appointments to plead the case. But, the date on the visa issued that day was September 1, 2001. Ten days later was the 9/11 terrorist attack on New York City. If John hadn't gotten Miquette out of Haiti before 9/11, when all the rules changed, she would never have made it back to the U.S.

After the appointment, out on the sidewalk, Miquette went ballistic—hugging, kissing, screaming. "Yes, Yes, Yes!"

Now I Can Die In Peace

After the appointment, everybody met at the Guest House. Miquette had arranged the reunion. Cleuis had not been at the airport when the Lees arrived and this was the first time he had seen his daughters Farah and Cherline in 12 years. Through Miquette, Cleuis said "They are so beautiful. Thank you. Now I can die in peace." This statement was remindful of the dramatic "nunc demittus." Old Simeon had been assured by the Holy Spirit that he would not die before he had seen the Lord's promised Messiah. Simeon, led by the Spirit, was at the temple when Joseph and Mary presented baby Jesus for the ceremony of purification. Simeon took the child in his arms and gave thanks to God. "Now, Lord you have kept your promise, and you may let your servant go in peace. With my own eyes I have seen your salvation . . ." (Luke 2:21-35)

The girls' brother Isaac was there. Twelve years earlier, Isaac, now about 29, the older brother, was broken hearted when he came home and found his two younger sisters, Farah and Cherline, had been given up for adoption.

Cherline's dad, Chavanne, was a school teacher. He made a long trip from northern Haiti to get to the reunion to meet Cherline. He said his other children were smart like Cherline. He showed pictures and pointed out that like Cherline, they had strong legs like the soccer players they all were. Chevon impressed the Lees as a tender, loving parent. He was a young man, in his 30's who looked muscular, strong and healthy. Yet, he died of natural causes (no other information) within the next year. In the fall of 2012, Cherline entered medical school at the University of Wisconsin in Madison. Why medical school? Partly because her father in Haiti died young without medical care. Cherline hopes to do a medical rotation in Haiti. Gladys Sylvestre Thomas says she will be welcome at her hospital. On the last day in Haiti, Miquette arranged another gathering (but at a slightly larger home than the one John Lee visited ten years earlier) where family members assembled outside in a circle. Each family member expressed thanks and appreciation to the Lees for all they had done for the family. The Lees were moved by the graciousness of the family, still living in the midst of poverty. The Lee family, returning to the U.S. by plane the next day, agreed that their adoptions, assistance and connection with the Denies in Haiti was by far the best thing they had ever done as a family.

CHAPTER 7

OAK GROVE—YOU'RE A GROVER NOW

*"It was only high school after all,
definitely one of the most bizarre periods
in a person's life. How anyone can come through
that time well adjusted on any level
is an absolute miracle."*

—*E.A. Bucchianeri*

The Oak Grove Lutheran School is a private school in Fargo, North Dakota, 50 miles west of Detroit Lakes offering classes from pre-kindergarten through 12th grade for approximately 400 students. It is operated by the Evangelical Lutheran Church of America. Oak Grove was founded in 1906, operating out of a one-shack school house that was intended primarily as a Christian school for Norwegian girls living in the rural areas. Now it is co-ed. Classes at Oak Grove have a student to teacher ratio of about 12 to 1. Approximately 96% of Oak Grove graduates pursue degrees in higher education.

Miquette noticed immediately that Oak Grove was much more diverse than Detroit Lakes. Included were foreign students from Russia, Japan and Yugoslavia. There were two black girls from Africa in her senior class of 32 students.

At Oak Grove, Miquette decided she had been too meek, too shy in Detroit Lakes and had to be more outgoing and get involved if she was going to get anywhere. She realized that many students at DLHS had been very casual, almost indifferent about education and were just sliding by. At Oak Grove there was a higher level of student commitment and attitude. It was an eye opener for her—a shock. So she decided to turn a new page in her own attitude. In her graduating class at Oak Grove, all but one student went on to college.

Miquette had the additional advantage of living with and being tutored by campus Pastor Anne Hokenstad. At Oak Grove international students do not live in dormitories, they live with adults and families. Pastor Hokenstad had three equal duties: teacher of religious studies, spiritual counsellor and administrator of religious programs. She served at Oak Grove from 1997 through 2004.

Miquette was continuing her struggle with English. As a former English teacher, Pastor Hokenstad was able to tutor her. She says Miquette worked hard on her English and on her homework in general. She demonstrated a determination, a clear sense of purpose—to return to Haiti as a nurse.

Miquette was plagued by nightmares while she was at Oak Grove, just as she had been at Detroit Lakes with the Lees. She would scream and beat the walls. When Hokenstad tried to calm her down, Miquette told her of being chased by robbers, people were coming after her in the middle of the night. It was a terrifying, recurring dream.

Anne said Miquette was an excellent cook and treated her mentor with her favorite Haitian dishes: rice and beans with cloves, onions and coconut milk, Haitian chicken, and for breakfast, a blend of chopped up green and red peppers, onion and red sauce over scrambled eggs.

Anne remembers Miquette's laughter and joy of life. She says as the year went along, her confidence and resilience grew dramatically. She was comfortable being older than most of her classmates (partly because she had learned to keep her mouth shut about her age) and was becoming acclimated to holding her own in our culture. She says Miquette showed "incredible faith that was always vivid and alive."

Pastor Hokenstad is now married, presently serving a church in Oakdale, Minnesota and writing her thesis in pursuit of a Doctor of Ministry degree at Luther Seminary in St. Paul.

Miquette especially remembers her geometry teacher at Oak Grove, Mr. Langseth. He was patient, kind and helpful, while expressing great curiosity about Haiti. She felt he cared about her as a person.

As an example of Miquette's "stepping out" attitude at Oak Grove, she went to the prom. She hadn't gone to the prom at Detroit Lakes and when prom rolled around at Oak Grove, a guy named Jordan asked her to go with him. She said yes, and they had a good time. She paid for her flowers by doing some extra jobs for Anne—washing windows, and other chores. Hokenstad was pleased that Miquette was exposed to that American tradition. Her natural beauty seemed to shine through at that time.

The Departed Were Turning Over In Their Graves

Miquette took behind the wheel drivers training at Oak Grove. She paid the extra fee by baby-sitting. One time, returning to Detroit Lakes with John Lee, he suggested they stop at the Eksjo church yard near Lake Park to practice. They were driving John's Toyota T-100 pickup with a straight stick (manual transmission). When Miquette let out the clutch, she pushed the accelerator all the way to the floor and the pickup rocketed ahead, gravel flying. Miquette was screaming. She was gripping the steering wheel. John hollered "take your foot off the gas." But Miquette was in a panic and she kept her foot down. Finally John reached down, pulled her foot off the gas and placed it on the brake. Miquette kept pushing, but now she was slamming on the brake. The truck lurched to a stop just a few feet from the cemetery gravestones. The departed were turning over in their graves.

When Miquette graduated, she needed a driver's license to get to and from her jobs. She took a written test on a machine. She failed it. John tutored her on procedure and terminology and she passed it the second time. That made her eligible for her behind-the-wheel test. She failed that because she couldn't handle parallel parking.

You Can't Fail Me

The second time she took the behind-the-wheel, she stopped at a stop sign at a blind corner. When she started again, she surged into the intersection. At the end of the test the testing officer told her she had failed the driving test because, after stopping, she should have crept into that intersection—it was not safe to just surge out. Miquette had a short deadline for getting her license and she "lost it" when she was told she had failed. She cried and wailed, she threw her head back and forth and it actually hit the horn and honked. "You can't fail me," she pleaded "I promise to creep into that intersection for the rest of my life." This shouldn't happen, but the testing officer caved in, changed his mind and passed her. Determination gets results.

The year at Oak Grove was a good year for her. She enjoyed her classes, sang on the choir, was active socially, worked hard, wrote many good papers and got good grades—good enough to get into Concordia College.

CHAPTER 8

CONCORDIA COLLEGE— YOU'RE A COBBER NOW

"There are obviously two educations. One should teach us how to make a living and the other how to live."

—James Treslow Adams

Concordia College is a highly regarded private coeducational liberal arts institution in Moorhead, Minnesota, founded by Norwegian settlers in the Red River Valley in 1891. The college, associated with the Evangelical Lutheran Church of America, has an enrollment of approximately 2,800 students.

The students, alumni, staff and athletic teams of Concordia are all known as "Cobbers." There is a story behind that name that may not need to be told, but it will be told anyway. In the Yiddish dialogue of Hebrew, a Cobber is a friend, comrade or good companion, but the Hebrew language has nothing to do with the Concordia Cobbers. Back when the college was founded, it was on the edge of Moorhead surrounded by cornfields. When urban-types came to compete with Concordia they slurred the predominately Norwegian farm boys from Concordia calling them "corncobs." The name stuck and in 1932, the Concordia boys, girls, teams and even the yearbook became Cobbers. The team logo is a snarling cob of corn.

In 2009, ESPN, the total sports network, listed the top 10 college teams with the most quirky nicknames. The Cobbers came in at number two. At the top of the list were the Banana Slugs of the University of California, Santa Cruz.

Recently, a group of Concordia students, along with their Mascot, Kernal Cobb, showed up at the Corn Palace in Mitchell, South Dakota and challenged the idea that the University of Nebraska could have a team named the Cornhuskers. The following corny challenge was issued by the Kernel: "They have no right to husk our corn! Upon their defeat we will be the only corn-themed team in all of college sports! Soon the day will come when we announce to the world, Venimus Frumentum, Vedimus Frumentum, Vcimus Frumentum! (We came to the corn, we saw the corn, we conquered the corn.)"

Miquette was dropped off at her Hoyum Hall dorm by John and Mary Lee to begin her college career. She was excited—she says college was new territory where none of her family had ever been. She said to herself, "I'm going to take every opportunity available to me here. I'm going to do my very best here on my own." Miquette Denie never became a Cobber fanatic, but she did wear the required corn colored freshman beanie upon her arrival.

Foreign students applying for college admission have an additional hurdle to get over. It's the TOEFL (Test Of English as a Foreign Language) test, a computer exercise to evaluate the ability of an individual to understand English in an academic setting. It's a tough, tricky test that may, for example, challenge the student to distinguish between further and farther in different situations. It would be difficult for American students. She didn't pass the first time. Sample practice tests are available and Miquette and John Lee worked through some together. She took the test at Minnesota State University Moorhead and passed the second time.

John Lee worked hard to put together a financial package that would take care of Miquette's expenses attending Concordia. It was done with a small Concordia Scholarship, Rotary assistance and Lee family funds (at one time, Miquette and the four Lee children were all in college or seminary at the same time). It was a financial struggle, requiring Miquette to work at the front desk at her dormitory and later, as a resident assistant (R.A.) at her residence, which covered housing. Other foreign students though, had even more of a struggle. When Miquette talked to them, she realized that almost all of them had student loans, which she did not have.

After her "One Step Forward" exercise, Miquette realized what she had always expected—that she was one of the poorest kids at Concordia. She said that even the poorest kids from Tanzania were not as poor as she was. But she had more financial backing. Though she was still somewhat embarrassed by her circumstances, she was not intimidated. She was encouraged that she was about to start a journey to change the course of her life.

Miquette worked at the student cafeteria at the beginning of her freshman year. She was amazed at the enormity of the place and the amount of available food. Her duties were in the kitchen where she was shocked by the waste—leftovers and totally untouched food. Because of health regulations, once the food was out, even if untouched, it had to be dumped. Washing dishes, she kept thinking about the huge numbers of Haitian people, or even struggling students, who could be fed by the food being wasted. This became a big issue for her and she stopped working there for that reason.

The bookstore was an exciting first adventure. Books all over the place—thousands of them. She spent almost $3000 on books right off the bat. She was converting dollars to Haitian Gourdes in her mind and the total was staggering.

The year was a good year, starting with "C" beanies for freshman and interesting, stimulating classes. She was impressed by her professors and fellow students. She felt her English was adequate because of her year at Oak Grove. In addition, Concordia had tutors for English as a second language at a tutoring center.

Miquette sang in the women's choir her freshman year, but dropped choir after that because of the need to focus on her very intense nursing program. Getting into nursing was not a cinch. Only about 20-22 students were accepted into the program each year, so admission was a big deal. Her sights were set on bringing a nursing degree back to Haiti.

Miquette was happy there were so many international students at Concordia. They all arrived two or three days earlier than the other students. Some were even older than she was—she said it was awesome that she was no longer the oldest.

John Lee was on the staff of the Bishop of the Northwestern Minnesota Synod of the Evangelical Lutheran Church of America (ELCA) while Miquette was enrolled at Concordia. The college made office space available to the ELCA so Lee was on campus. Miquette dropped in to see him often, just to visit or to connect for a weekend ride back to Detroit Lakes. These were fun times for Lee.

During her second year at Concordia, Miquette was living at the International Building and working at the front desk at the Erickson and Hallet Hall checking ID's for students going in and out of the dorm. The advantage of this job was that she had time to do homework while on duty.

For pre-nursing students, the second semester of the second year is the time when pressure starts to mount. There is a nerve-wracking test before students can even enter the program. A portion of the test is an essay. Enrollment space in nursing is limited and Miquette heard she was near the cutoff line. She had no plan B. She thinks her essay, not her grades, got her over the hump. Her essay included her dream to return to Haiti to provide quality nursing care for her people. She said "If I am admitted to the program, it will be the best decision you ever make. My heart is in this." Well, of course, she was admitted.

There was a crisis in Miquette's junior year. It was nursing, full speed ahead. But it was hard—especially the chemistry. Miquette had to put in many more hours of study than her classmates. She got discouraged. She called the Lees and said she wanted to drop out of nursing and become a social worker. "My friends are out having a good time while I'm working hard and struggling long hours to grasp this stuff" she said. She was crying. This was the first time the Lees had ever heard Miquette say she couldn't do something.

Miquette met with John and Mary Lee in a state of depression. They sat on the bed in Miquette's room and talked it out. The Lees were low key but firm in talking about Miquette's goals. They reminded her of her original plan, that nursing and returning to Haiti had been her goal since she was a junior in high school and that they had told the U.S. Consul General she would be coming back to Haiti as a nurse. They told her she probably couldn't be self-supporting in Haiti with a social work degree. Nurses are so needed in Haiti. Again, Miquette was crying. The Lees told her if she needed tutoring they would arrange it. Miquette never said she definitely would quit nursing, so the Lees urged her to stick with it and see if she could work it out. At the end, Miquette said "We'll see." She says she "got back on the horse" determined to make it. She said her teachers and classmates were so helpful, even though they didn't realize she had been at a point of crisis.

Before the junior year was over, the tide had turned. When the program moved into the "practicum" stage—actually working with real people and not simply academic studies, Miquette's game perked up. She loved the person-to-person contact and discovered she was good at it. Simply, she was a people person.

In addition, her professors discovered that Miquette was a resource person. When it came to diseases like rickets, malaria and tuberculosis, Miquette knew symptoms and treatment because of actual experience in Haiti. Both professors and classmates turned to her for her practical knowledge and experience. The practicum experience and first hand medical background made the last year and a half of nursing studies much more pleasant for her.

Dr. Jack Rydell, now Director of Nursing Studies at Concordia College, was an assistant professor in his first year of teaching when Miquette was in her last year of nursing, 2005-2006. Before that, he had been Director of Patient Care at the Hospice of the Red River Valley for eight years. Dr. Rydell had Miquette in two classes, Nursing Roles and Issues and Nursing Management. He remembered Miquette well and paid her the ultimate compliment: "She was an authentic student." Rydell found her personable and engaging in class, interesting, respectful and highly motivated.

She was getting moral and spiritual support from the Haitian community in Fargo-Moorhead which was most helpful for her. Her best friend in the community was a Haitian woman by the name of Ortince who had lived in Fargo at least 10 years. Ortince showed her around and took her to a church of about 30-50 Haitian people with lots of kids. They even had a pot luck of Haitian foods which was wonderful for her.

When Miquette was cooking for her African friends, meals of rice, beans and Haitian chicken with sauce the friends were saying "This is what my grandmother used to make for us." This, in effect was linking the African culture with that of Haiti. Those recipes had undoubtedly come to Haiti with the slaves hundreds of years before.

She Kissed Her Diploma

All the toughest battles had been fought and won. Miquette's senior year at Concordia came and went and it was time for graduation. When that day arrived, her mother's friend, Carmel Wagnac, who had helped support Miquette as a student in Haiti when tuition funds were short, came all the way from Chicago with her nephew for the graduation. Miquette said Carmel was a strong, loyal, amazing woman. The Lees were there too, of course—proud of what Miquette had achieved.

Miquette remembers being greatly impressed by the commencement speaker at the graduation ceremony, Rev. Dr. Donald Messer, Theologian, Iliff School of Theology. The speaker snapped his fingers every three seconds and told the graduates that every three seconds someone somewhere was dying because of lack of water, lack of health care and lack of education. She said the address was "amazing and challenging" and fueled her passion to return to Haiti to provide health care and support education. The title of the address was "Every Three Seconds."

When Miquette got her diploma, she kissed it. "It was a wonderful feeling" she says.

Dream Bigger Dreams

Dr. William Craft, President of Concordia College since 2011, has spoken at length with Miquette several times since her graduation and says "I love to tell Miquette's story—it's a compelling story." President Craft the Lutheran concept of vocation is that "We are called as children of God and are sent forth to serve as called."

As a student, Miquette dreamed of returning to Haiti to establish a program for educating poor Haitian children. This was her call and she heard it clearly. And this is exactly what she is doing now. Craft asked Miquette what difference Concordia has made in her life, and loved her answer: "Concordia taught me to dream bigger dreams."

Craft observes that in an age where graduates are filled with anxieties about getting a job and earning a paycheck, Miquette was always thinking beyond her diploma. And she has grown as a thinker since her graduation as she has added depth and substance to her original vision and has impressed him deeply as a shining example of "doing for others."

CHAPTER 9

THE GRADUATE—COUNTDOWN TO LAUNCH

"He who opens a school door, closes a prison."
—Victor Hugo

Miquette had worked at St. Mary's Hospital in Detroit Lakes as a paid "student intern" the summer before her fourth year of nursing studies and St. Mary's was waiting for her to return as an RN. After graduation she was a "graduate intern" until she passed her boards. She took her nursing board examinations in June of that summer after graduation. The test was computer/multiple choice and English was still an occasional hurdle for her. She didn't pass. But between the first board test and the second, in August, she stopped working and stayed home (at Lee's, rent free—"save your money for Haiti") and studied. More intense review and homework followed and she took the boards again, totally confident, and passed.

The idea of starting an educational foundation was in her heart and mind and became a subject of some discussion with key people at Concordia. An advisor there suggested she attend a non-profit seminar in St. Paul called "Non-Profit 101." John Lee agreed and attended with her, the purpose being achieving tax recognition as a 501(c)(3) organization so donors could deduct their gifts. As a result of the seminar her thinking became even more focused.

Rev. Dave Peterson is a pastor of First Lutheran Church in Detroit Lakes, MN. Miquette is a member of First Lutheran. Pastor Peterson became acquainted with Miquette through John and Mary Lee, also members of First Lutheran, and knew her when she worked at the St. Mary's Hospital and Emmanuel Nursing Home in Detroit Lakes after her graduation from Concordia College.

When she was working at Emmanuel, Miquette came to Peterson and told him that God's plan for her was to return to her native Haiti to establish a scholarship program for poor Haitian children because education was the path out of poverty.

It was obvious to Peterson that Miquette had given her decision a good deal of thought and prayer and had done her homework. Her mission that day was to get some advice or assistance in forming a non-profit organization to receive donations and start funding her vision. She wasn't going off "half-cocked"—she was determined to do diligent preparation and organizational work before starting to seek contributions.

She asked Peterson two specific questions:
Would First Lutheran Church act as a temporary financial agent for her project, TeacHaiti, until it could establish its own Federal Code tax exempt 501(c)(3) status making donations deductible? Would Pastor Peterson be willing to be on the first board of directors of TeacHaiti to help get the organization off the ground?

The answer to the first question was yes. First Lutheran had 501(c)(3) status and the Church Vision Council later agreed to assist TeacHaiti by acting as temporary financial agent. All receipts would be deposited in a separate, special account and all disbursements from that account would be duly recorded.

The answer to the second question was a suggestion by Pastor Peterson. Because of his limited business experience, he recommended a person whose wide-ranging experience and sound business judgment he respected: Tom Klyve. Klyve had served on the First Lutheran Vision Council and had impressed Peterson and the entire council with his sharp questions, detailed analysis, common sense and focused decision making as well as his faith and concern about the needs of others. Other supporters had also endorsed Klyve.

Before he knew it, TeacHaiti was up and running with Tom Klyve on the board and contributions were being deposited into the special account.

When she passed her exam, she returned to St. Mary's working full-time as an RN. She worked there and at Emmanuel from August 2006 until June 2007 when she returned to Haiti. During that year she was talking to the people she was working with at St. Mary's and Emmanuel, her friends and other people about her TeacHaiti dreams. She wanted to help educate Haitian children the way the Lees had helped educate her. By 2007 she was going to clubs and churches and giving talks. John Lee went to a pastors conference at Fair Hills Resort and told the pastors assembled there they could expect to hear from Miquette and they did. Her original goal was to raise $3000 for 10 student scholarships. The Lee 2007 calendar shows that Miquette spoke to a church group in Hoffman, Minnesota, the Bakke, Lund and Richwood Churches (3 point rural congregation) on March 11th, Trinity Lutheran of Detroit Lakes on March 18th, and First Lutheran of Detroit Lakes on March 25th. The ball was rolling. On April 2nd and April 25th a TeacHaiti advisory was meeting to make plans to organize a support group. Miquette gave another talk to the Osage, Minnesota Women of the Lutheran Church of America. She adjusted the target amount to $30,000 and the money kept coming. The more people she talked to, the more pledges she got.

Miquette had also told her family in Haiti about the vision. They were proud and happy, but the word got out and before long, scores of families were waiting to be interviewed because they had children they hoped could go to Miquette's schools. Ultimately, $30,000 was raised and when Miquette returned to Haiti she negotiated with private schools, achieved discounts, leveraged the money and arranged for 41 scholarships starting in September 2007. Many stood in line to be among the chosen. Family interviews followed and student report cards were reviewed. Those awarded scholarships were all the way from first grade through high school. All 41 lived in Port au Prince.

In January of 2007, Miquette and John Lee traveled with a volunteer mission group to Ocean Springs, Mississippi, to assist in the Hurricane Katrina clean-up effort. John led the group. Miquette met Dr. Clayton Jensen, a Concordia Graduate in 1954, a member of the group, who later offered volunteer services in Haiti. When they met, they saw one another's Concordia College rings and made a big fuss about it as C-ring corncobbers are required by tradition to always do.

Dr. Jensen, duly impressed, volunteered to do a TeacHaiti mission trip in January, 2012, as described in Chapter 20.

Finally, June 11 of 2007, John Lee packed a backpack for himself and Miquette packed two suitcases (she loved shoes then and still does) to return to Haiti where Miquette was to begin her career in her native land. Miquette said John was with her when she came to America and he should be with her when she returned to Haiti.

CHAPTER 10

BACK TO THE MOTHERLAND

"Beginnings are often scary, endings are usually sad,
but it's what's in the middle that counts.
So just give hope a chance to float up—and it will."

—*Steven Rogers, HOPE FLOATS*

Miquette had a job lined up even before she left America. It was with a medical non-profit group. She had been hired after an interview in Minneapolis to assist in the groundwork of establishing a clinic and hospital in the coastal city of Les Cayes (pronounced la kay) in southern Haiti. John Lee and Miquette's mother, Rose flew with Miquette down to Les Cayes to begin her duties. Miquette had a supply of donated medical supplies from St. Mary's Hospital in Detroit Lakes.

Les Cayes, with miles of sandy beaches on the Caribbean, was moving in the direction of reestablishing the Haitian tourist trade, certainly a worthwhile endeavor. And the goal of establishing a new clinic and hospital was also worthwhile, as was the fighting of poverty. But the job in Les Cayes was not a fit for Miquette. While Les Cayes was within three hours of Port au Prince, it was a world away from the neighborhood and the children Miquette felt called to serve. So, after a year in Les Cayes, she returned to Port au Prince.

At this point, let us look at where Haiti stood among its Caribbean neighbors as Miquette was searching for and establishing her role among her people. The following table, published by the National Geographic Family Reference Atlas of the World, Second Edition, shows comparative statistics relating to population, literacy, life expectancy and gross domestic product per capita in the Caribbean: Bermuda, Cayman Islands, Cuba, Dominican Republic, Jamaica, Puerto Rico and Haiti in 2007.

	Population	Literacy	Life Expectancy	Gross Domestic Production
Bermuda	62,000	98%	77 years	$64,749
Cayman Islands	44,000	98%	79 years	38,594
Cuba	11,275,000	97%	77 years	3,059
Dominican Republic	8,862,000	85%	68 years	2,706
Jamaica	2,666,000	88%	73 years	3,225
Puerto Rico	3,912,000	94%	77 years	21,481
Haiti	8,288,000	53%	52 years	471

Could the challenge be any clearer? Fortunately, upon her return to Port au Prince, Miquette found the job perfectly suited to her life experiences and education. She was hired as school nurse and biology teacher at the Quisqueya Christian School in Port au Prince. Quisqueya is a private school where the children attending came from families that can afford to send them there. But her duties left her with enough personal time to address her mission—educating the poor kids in Haiti.

The money she had raised in Minnesota was used to place children in already-established private schools starting with the 2007-2008 school year. She was able to place 41 students with the money raised for 30 by negotiating with the schools (e.g. "If I send six kids to your school, can we agree that you will take them for ¾ what you're asking?") It worked, and the program was rolling.

Miquette returned to Detroit Lakes each summer to tell the Rotary Club, Kiwanis, the churches, library clubs and whoever would listen to her about the children, the need and the program. She was on a regular speaking circuit. She had to keep the support coming and add to it. That first summer back, 2008, the number of sponsors jumped to 90, again negotiated and leveraged by Miquette to finance 101 scholarships for the 2008-2009 school year. The year after that, 2009-2010, 150 scholarships were awarded. The program was successful and growing.

Then, in January of 2010, the great earthquake centered in Port au Prince destroyed many of the school buildings and education in the capital city came to a near standstill. Before the quake, the TeacHaiti board had discussed establishing its own school as part of the overall scholarship program. The consensus was "Yes, maybe 10 years down the road." But everything had changed. A head count showed about 60 TeacHaiti children grades 1-4, many in tents in the Delmas neighborhood, now had no school to attend. The board reconsidered the question and decided the time was "here and now" to establish its own classrooms.

Miquette's sister, Sandra, owned a small block building in the neighborhood, for lease but empty. The board decided to open a school in the building and sent a team of six in August, 2010, with books, pencils, tablets, school supplies and paint brushes to shape the building up, get the toilets flushing, and get it ready for grades 1-4 in September. Money came from the Fairfax Community Church group in Fairfax, Virginia, and Detroit Lakes and the $2,000 needed to do the quick fix was available almost overnight. Miquette said the little school "was meant to be." This was the birth of the School of Hope.

CHAPTER 11

EDUCATION IN HAITI

"Learning to read is probably the most difficult and revolutionary thing that happens to the human brain, and if you don't believe that, watch an illiterate adult try to do it."

—John Steinbeck

The story of education in Haiti is a long, sad tale in search of a happy ending. Haiti's literacy rate is only about 53% (55% for males and 51% for females) compared with the 90% average literacy rate for Latin American and Caribbean countries.

International private schools (run by Canadians, French or Americans) and church-run schools educate 90% of students. Haiti has 15,200 primary schools of which only 10% are public schools.

The original constitution of 1805 provided that "education should be free" and primary education shall be compulsory. Public education for all was guaranteed by the revised constitution of 1807. Finally, the constitution was amended in 1987 to provide that "education shall be the right of every citizen." The government attempted to expand access to public education in the 1940's but this was halted during the Duvalier era. Qualified teachers actually left Haiti during the Duvalier years because of repression by both Pappa Doc and Baby Doc Duvalier, but the development of private schools was accelerated because of a rule promulgated by Baby Doc that any new church was required to build an affiliated school.

Despite the constitutional provision requiring public education free to all people, the Haitian government has been unable to provide what it requires. Only 67% of eligible children enroll for elementary school. Of these, only 70% continue on to third grade. This means that nearly 33% of children between the ages of 6 and 12 (600,000 children) do not attend school at all. This percentage climbs to 40% for children ages 12 to 15 or approximately one million children. Ultimately 60% of children drop out of school before receiving a primary education certificate. While the mandated age for entering the first grade is 6, the average age for beginning students is 10 and students in grade six average 16 years old. This pattern is the same as when Miquette Denie was a student and it continues to this day. Why? The government has provided very few public schools, so the poor are unable to attend without outside help.

Among private schools, there are three main types. The most numerous are for-profit schools run by entrepreneurs. These schools have few, if any, books and are generally run by unqualified teachers and school directors. They are often known as "lottery schools" because only by chance do the children learn anything. The second type is private schools run by religious organizations such as Catholic or Evangelical churches and some nonsectarian schools. These schools generally offer a better quality of education than the for-profit schools, but still the quality is questionable depending on the professional qualifications of staff. The School of Hope would be this category of schools but superior to most for reasons set forth in Chapter 12. The third type of private school is the "community school" financed by whatever funds the local community can scratch up. They tend to be the lowest quality of the three, but their fees are low. Three quarters of the private schools operate with no certification or license from the Ministry of Education, meaning that anyone can open a school at any level of education, recruit students and hire teachers without having to meet any minimum standards.

There is a handful of private schools, mostly in Port au Prince, which are accessible to the rich (except for limited scholarship fund opportunities) that offer education with relatively high standards. The Quisqueya Christian School is one such school. Only the privileged few attend these schools.

It gets worse as the process advances from primary education to secondary. Less than 22% of children move up from elementary to secondary education. How available is secondary education? Of the approximately 2,190 secondary schools in Haiti, 90.5% are private and 78% of those are in urban areas, giving rural children even less access to an education. Only 20% of government spending reaches rural areas where 70% of Haiti's population is found.

Higher education consists of four regional public universities including the State University of Haiti and 4 other public institutions and a growing number of private institutions. Public education is relatively free for the few who have advanced that far. In addition to university education, vocational education is available for secondary students who have successfully completed 10 years. Family centers have programs in clothing, cooking and household arts for people who have not completed elementary education.

The 2010 earthquake made a horrible situation even worse. Nearly 4,200 schools were destroyed, affecting roughly half of all enrolled students at all levels and 90% of all Port au Prince Students. Schools minimally or not structurally damaged were closed for many months. Some reopened in tents and temporary shelters. Many students, teachers and administrators were injured or killed.

Just after the earthquake, about a half million children under the age of 18 were living on the streets, in crowded orphanages or makeshift camps—separated from their families and threatened by hunger, disease, sexual assault and even modern-day slave trade. Ten weeks after the quake, many were still uncertain of food or shelter and for families with missing children, it was impossible to know who was still living and who was dead.

The earthquake was a precipitating event for the construction of the School of Hope. Many schools where TeacHaiti scholarship students were enrolled were destroyed, though no TeacHaiti children were killed. It was decided that TeacHaiti should establish a school of its own for displaced students while continuing to provide scholarship support for students in undamaged schools. In August of 2010, a team of six TeacHaiti volunteers from Detroit Lakes and Hoffman, Minnesota arrived Port au Prince with books and school supplies to work in painting, furnishing and refurbishing a rented home to convert into classrooms for grades 1-4.

CHAPTER 12

THE TEACHAITI PROGRAM

"Kids don't remember what you try to teach them.
They remember what you are."

—*Jim Hensen*

To summarize the TeacHaiti program, it is a program to support the wellbeing of Haitian children, helping to improve literacy and health so that they may emerge from poverty. This is done by providing scholarships and other funding to deserving and motivated children and young adults with quality education and improved healthcare within a safe environment. The organization is incorporated as a Minnesota non-profit corporation and has obtained 501(3)(c) tax status so that contributions may be deducted by donors.

Since the beginning, the 2007-2008 school year, the number of students benefiting from TeacHaiti assistance has been as follows:

School Year	Students
2007-2008	41
2008-2009	108
2009-2010	169
2010-2011	184
2011-2012	302
2012-2013	320
2013-2014	370

For the first three years, scholarships were provided in private schools not operated by TeacHaiti. In the earthquake of January 2010, many of those schools were destroyed and classes stopped, although no TeacHaiti students lost their lives. In order to continue the education of these children, TeacHaiti based and opened its own school for the 2010-2011 school year, but continued to help fund children in other private schools. The new school is known as the School of Hope. There are several schools of hope in Port au Prince, but only one is operated by TeacHaiti.

Educating the mind without educating the heart
is no education at all
—Aristotle
Poster in 6th grade classroom at School of Hope

The School of Hope opened in September, 2010 with 60 scholarship children, grades K-4. All first graders had been TeacHaiti-sponsored kindergarten children. The program included three years of kindergarten, and one year of pre-school.

The following year, swamped with requests from families for admission to all grades, TeacHaiti initiated entrance exams for new students. The tests measured age, proficiency levels for the applicable grade and weaknesses in need of remedy. The tests were tailor-made by the TeacHaiti principals using standards from other schools and selected TeacHaiti benchmarks.

The School of Hope has its own program, not the same as the other TeacHaiti sponsored schools. Of the 370 students presently in TeacHaiti schools, 190 are in the School of Hope and 180 are in other schools. In addition 15 college students are being sponsored. The average cost of a college student in $4000 each year. The School of Hope offered only grades 1-4 in its first year. The following year, the program was expanded to include K-5. Annual expansions have brought the school to its current program which includes children starting at age three in a three year kindergarten program and grades 1-6. Space limitations at present prevent teaching students at the School of Hope beyond 6th grade. These students go to scattered schools in the neighborhood, still being sponsored by TeacHaiti.

Additional space has been rented and remodeled across the street from the original School of Hope where classes have been held since the beginning of the 2012-2013 school year. A small playground is available at the newer facility. The playground, in bright colors, was paid for, built and painted in bright colors by a group from Fairfax Community Church in Fairfax, Virginia, lead by Bill Zink.

Before children are admitted into the School of Hope, they are given proficiency tests developed by the faculty to be assured they have the ability to succeed at their age and grade level.

Although you will find references throughout the faculty discussion of this book, here is a summary of what the School of Hope provides:

- Students must maintain a B average.
- A holistic philosophy – they treat the children as their own, with emphasis on love and respect for the whole child and his or her total needs.
- One nutritious meal each day.
- Health and hygiene training.

- English is taught to all students.

- French is taught to all students.

- There is no corporal punishment – fear is not considered an educational tool.

- Christian devotions 8:00-9:00 every Friday. Bible classes in the classroom in French and Creole.

- Memorization discouraged—students are encouraged to understand by asking questions.

- Teaching by example.

- Sex education in 6th grade – boys and girls together.

- Morality training in 6th grade.

- Computer training starting in 4th grade.

- Parents must give service to the school, including cleaning, preparing lunch, serving food.

- Quarterly meetings between parents and staff.

- Parents committee.

For the school year 2013-2014, TeacHaiti sponsors 370 students of all ages and grades, including 13 college students. Of these, 190 are located in the School of Hope, some in the original school-rooms, and many across the street in a newer facility that includes some brightly painted playground equipment.

The hiring of staff personnel by the School of Hope starts with a resume and references. Those clearing that hurdle are given a written test in French requiring the applicants to express their goals and hobbies, reading habits, books read, and what they can bring to the school. They are scored based on grammar, structure, values, articulation and general writing skills. For those still in consideration, an oral interview by a three person committee consisting of Miquette, Pascale Girault and Daniele Jules (Interviews of Pascale and Daniele are in Chapter 16.). The successful candidates are hired. In the past few years, one principal and one teacher have been dismissed for poor performance. The professional staff at the School of Hope for the year 2013-2014 consists of one bookkeeper, one principal and 12 teachers directing the learning of children in one year of pre-school, three years of kindergarten and grades 1-6.

TeacHaiti also sponsors children in 10 schools at St. Michel, two schools in Les Cayes and four schools in Gonaives. The schools are monitored through a review of passing grades in national exams, though the principals and teachers in those schools have not been selected and hired by TeacHaiti. Chantal Denie, secretary and coordinator at the School of Hope, described by Miquette as smart, able, responsible, trustworthy, and the "backbone" of the School of Hope, personally delivers scholarship money (remember, Haiti has no postal system) and monitors the operation of those schools.

All of the teachers in the School of Hope have university degrees (except one who is in the process of finishing hers) which is unusual for schools in Haiti. Although Haitian schools are required to be licensed by the Minister of Education, the School of Hope is still waiting for its license. There is no follow up and no enforcement by the ministry. However the Minister of Education has visited the school several times and has said "I wish this school were close to me, I'd send my kids here."

In the last national exam given after the 6th grade, 100% of School of Hope children passed. These exams follow the 6th, 8th, 11th and 12th grades. In other TeacHaiti schools 54 of 57 passed.

The vision for the future of TeacHaiti is for a Port au Prince campus that would have not only the primary school, but a vocational school and a clinic. Also the same combination in St. Michel where the need is even greater. Classes in St. Michel in 2013 are conducted in a tent for 40 children. The need there and the eagerness to participate are demonstrated by the children outside the tent, looking and wishing to be there. But a permanent school in St. Michel is more attainable because land prices in Port au Prince are so much higher.

The TeacHaiti board has approved the construction of a new school in St. Michel, pending the raising of the necessary funds. It is presently estimated that the cost of construction of a new school there would be $175,000.00. Highly motivated supporters from Fairfax, Virginia and Bedford, Pennsylvania are moving in the direction of raising the money and building the school. There is a good chance all this could be accomplished by the end of 2015.

Once the St. Michel School has been built, it will be operated by Haitians, the same as the School of Hope and other schools where TeacHaiti students are enrolled.

The interviewer raised the question of what would become of the TeacHaiti mission if Miquette were to meet an untimely disability or death. Miquette answers with confidence. She has total faith that Chantal Denie, the bookkeeper and coordinator, has a grasp of the School of Hope operation and the leadership ability to independently carry out the mission. The fundraising aspect, including appearing in America, meeting and speaking to supporters, would continue without interruption in the hands of Bilybert Audige, the School of Hope Coordinator (and teacher, translator, interpreter). However, past attempts to bring Audigo to the United States have not been successful, as his visa has been denied.

Interestingly, these discussions about the present and future direction of TeacHaiti were conducted on Saturday, December 7, 2013 sitting outside at a picnic table near the home of Miquette and Art on the Quisqueya Christian School campus in temperatures between 85-90 degrees with "Oh Come Let Us Adore Him" floating in from somewhere in the neighborhood.

FACULTY AND STAFF

BILLYBERT AUDIGE

 Billybert ("Bily") Audige is a 29 year old bachelor who speaks and teaches English and works as School Coordinator at the TeacHaiti School of Hope.

Bily finished high school at a private school in 2004 then completed his bachelor's degree in English and Economics at the State Haitian University in 2011. In high school, family finances were very tight and he often went to school from 8:00 a.m. to 2:00 p.m. without any food. When he did eat, he often shared a lunch with another student, a common practice in Haiti. But he received much encouragement from his mother who repeatedly told him that "You must succeed in life and you much study to succeed. If you don't know how to read or write you will have very few opportunities." (Haiti has no welfare system.)

Bily lost time between high school and college because of general chaos and political instability in the country that he blames on President Aristide. During that time he tutored and gave lessons to neighborhood children, getting paid by their parents, and helping his mother with the money earned.

The University was almost free, but it was very difficult to get in. There were limited openings and many candidates for those few openings with numerous entrance tests to sort out the applicants. The teachers were highly motivated and excellent. But if a student failed exams in the first year, the student was out.

Bily lost one year because of the earthquake. The school building collapsed and an entire year of the program, 2010 had to wait before classes resumed in 2011.

Most other elementary schools don't teach English, which isn't available until high school. But the School of Hope teaches English twice a week in grades one and two and three times a week in grades three through six. He says the School of Hope "is family."

The students enjoy the study of English. There are a number of reasons. Many visitors from the U.S. came to the school and ask questions in English. In addition English allows the children to learn about another culture, the American culture. The children now can name the President of the United Sates. Also, they are able to join in the singing of English songs in church. One 12 year old School of Hope student gives English lessons, for pay, to other children in the neighborhood, earning the equivalent of $3.00 each week which she turns over to her mother for food for her family. The children being tutored are probably students going to private schools where English is not being taught.

Stories circulate about the benefits of being able to read, write and speak English. One School of Hope student went to summer camp where questions to the students were in English. When she was able to answer, in English, she was awarded a prize—a book written in English.

Another English language success story is that a TeacHaiti student, a 5th grader named Caride Flor Aujour, was on the street and observed some American missionaries pass some laborers wearing hard hats working in the streets. The missionaries said "God Bless You" to the workers who didn't react because they had no idea what was being said. So the student interpreted for the workers, giving them the message in their native Creole. The workers smiled, waved and said thanks in Creole, which the student passed along to the missionaries in English. The missionaries were so impressed, they gave the little girl $5.00, an amazing amount of money to a poor Haitian kid. The money was passed along to the girl's mom for family expenses. Imagine, getting money just for knowing English.

There is a free summer camp each year for neighborhood children, including TeacHaiti children. A group from Washington, D.C. was there in the summer of 2012 leading a project of singing, crafts, storybooks, studying animals and fish. This camp is run like a Vacation Bible School day camp, but is not operated by TeacHaiti.

The School of Hope also teaches French, Creole (the native language of Haiti), history, geography, science, reading, math, health and has Bible classes in French and Creole as well as Christian devotions from 8:00-9:00 every Friday.

French is important because after the 4th grade, all students are required to take and pass a national exam before being allowed to pass to the 5th grade. Much of the exam is in French and without a background in French grammar, passing would be impossible. Most of the children do not speak French at home.

Bily feels the School of Hope is superior to many other private schools because the teachers are better educated and better trained. He said many of the other schools have teachers with 8th grade educations only. Also, many attempt to teach through memorization, but that doesn't lead to understanding. He says the teachers and students of the School of Hope are friends. While students in many Haitian schools are subjected to corporal punishment, no teacher at the School of Hope ever strikes a child. Bily says he was hit by his teachers when he was a student. Fear is not a part of the curriculum. Students are encouraged to ask questions and challenge their teachers and one another.

Bily explained the restavek arrangement as applying mostly to young girls from the country living with city families. For these girls, there is no acceptance into the family they live with, no education and limited food. The girls often get pregnant early and the few boys in the program end up with drug and/or alcohol problems. This is an arrangement that happens to children who have no education and it is a dead-end arrangement—no future.

Bily was on the 4th floor of a friend's house when the earthquake struck. He felt the rumble and fell flat on the floor where he rode it out. The building did not collapse. When the earth stopped shaking, he went outside and found buried and dead people. He lost a 14 year old sister in the quake when she was hit on the head by a falling concrete block. He said his mother is still crying over her daughter's death, and many in Port au Prince are still crying as well. Nobody can forget the disaster.

One of Bily's duties is to visit schools in Gonaives and St. Michel where TeacHaiti-sponsored students are enrolled, to observe and supervise, also to deliver the tuition. He says the schools in Port au Prince are at a higher level of performance than those out in the country.

Bily was working at the Quisqueya Christian School in Port au Prince as an interpreter and translator just after the earthquake when he met Miquette for the first time. He was impressed and inspired by her leadership. She hired him as a teacher for the School of Hope and she has made it clear that she expects the program to be conducted in a high quality fashion. He admires her drive and courage and is striving to follow her example of being educated in the U.S. and returning to Haiti.

This guy, Billybert Audige, is an impressive young man. Several days after the interview he sent supplementary materials that he wanted included in the interview notes. He says he would like to go to the U.S.A. and pursue further studies and possibly pick up an MBA, then return to Haiti to bring his experience and learning to his people. Could he be the next Miquette Denie?

When shown pictures of huge piles of snow and frosty trees in Minnesota, Bily admitted he had never seen snow or frost except in movies or pictures. Then he proved how little he, and probably most Haitians, know about ice, snow and winter, by asking of there was any water in snow. Then he asked where snow came from and how it got on the ground. He also asked questions about global warming.

Bily works part-time for the American Federation of Teachers (AFT) and the Vermont Medical Response Team (VMRT) as an interpreter and coordinator of the Vermont group's clinic project established in Port au Prince after the earthquake along with a trade union electrical company (CTST).

JEFFERSON DANIEL LALEAU

Mr. LaLeau is the 30 year old principal of the School of Hope. His job description includes recruiting teachers, organizing and coordinating classes, organizing activities, student discipline, parent contact and teaching. The 2013-2014 school year is his third at the School of Hope.

LaLeau says "we do what we love." He's the guy that students have to see when they're required to talk to the principal. He explains that children are playful and most of those who misbehave are intelligent, so they need to understand that while they're free, they must show respect for the school, the faculty and one another.

The school, as yet, has no sports program, though they'd love to have one. But the second, newer building in the School of Hope, across the street, has a playground where the children can swing, slide, jump-rope and play-soccer. This helps them run off energy. More soccer balls, hula-hoops, volley balls and space are needed, but budgets are tight and no more space is available at this time.

Mr. LaLeau studied communications and journalism for one year at the Haitian Center for Communications after he finished high school. His jobs since then have always been in education, as a primary school teacher and as a supervisor in high school. At the present time he is enrolled in a degree program in education at Crefima University. He attends on weekends and has completed one year of studies with three remaining.

He teaches three classes, a computer class to 4th graders, morality class to sixth graders and a sex education class, boys and girls together, all classes once a week. There is no special education as such, although there are students with learning disabilities who get special attention from their teachers and Mr. LaLeau reports progress to their parents.

The computer program makes use of laptop computers received from the Fairfax Community Church (FCC) in Fairfax, Virginia. Computer supplies will continue to be needed.

LaLeau has extensive contact with the parents of School of Hope students. All parents are expected to talk to the teachers and attend quarterly meetings with the principal and a parents committee. The role of the parents committee is to establish and maintain good relationships between the school, the parents and the children. The teachers and principal challenge the parents with questions about what they expect from the School of Hope and why their children should be part of the program. The parents are required to provide services to the school like cleaning, preparing lunch or serving the food.

Jefferson LaLeau believes the future of Haiti depends on education and that the future will hold few opportunities for illiterate children. He says educating is not an easy job but that it requires "working with your heart." He's proud to be part of the team at the School of Hope and is continually impressed and inspired by Miquette.

ROSEMANE CELY

When Miquette was a kindergarten student (called Enfantine II) in St. Michel, her teacher was a young woman by the name of Rosemane Cely. Ms. Cely remembers Miquette as being a bright, quiet learner, always eager to participate in everything.

Now Rosemane is a third grade teacher at the School of Hope. She conducts all classes in French, using Creole only when necessary to make explanations. She also teaches French Communications as a separate subject: vocabulary, grammar, reading, writing, spelling and French topics. She teaches another class called Creole Communications, covering the children's native Creole language in the same categories as her class in French Communications.

Rosemane has been teaching for 25 years because she loves to teach. She went through the 11th grade and still needs two more classes to finish high school which is 13 grades in Haiti. Then she studied for three years in an Education School for teacher's training. She has always been a teacher, including Bible School classes. When she was a student, she took seamstress training which she considers a practical skill she thinks the schools should still teach. When she retires she intends to use her seamstress skills in selling curtains, table cloths and clothes from Panama. Always thinking ahead, she would do this by home sales or a rented retail store.

Rosemane says one of the most important things that happens at the School of Hope every day is that the students are fed a lunch at noon. For some, this is the only meal of the day. They get a variety of foods, including a generous portion of rice with oisnon (onion) sauce and sauce pois (a Hawaiian dish made from the root of taro).

The feedback she gets from parents is that they love the School of Hope and are so thankful for the opportunity the school gives their children.

She says Miquette has a great heart and loves the children. She wants every one of them to have a bright future. She constantly encourages the teachers to improve their skills and get better and better.

Rosemane, a mother of two adult children, says God blessed her that she was not injured in the earthquake. But she has nightmares and the sounds of the quake still haunt her. She never sleeps with the bedroom door closed anymore—she wants a quick escape in the event of another quake.

CLAUDE PIERRE

Claude Pierre, wearing gray whiskers, a Los Angeles Angels baseball cap and a Children's Ministries Kidwell Park t-shirt, works at the School of Hope as a security officer and custodian. He has been employed at the school since 2010.

He first knew Miquette when she was a little girl living in St. Michel.

Miquette's grandmother was Claude's godmother.

Mr. Pierre was a farmer originally, but when farming became marginal for him, he left the St. Michel area. His first stop was at Carrefour Feuille where he worked from 1982-1990 as a mason. Then he moved to Delmas where he lives now. From 1990-2010 he worked at the Gertrude Bienamie orphanage, his duties being the same as at the School of Hope, except he also did jobs at the Gladys Guest House where he became acquainted with John and Mary Lee when they came to Port au Prince on their adoption mission. The Angels cap Claude was wearing was sent to him by people staying at the guest house.

MANUEL JEAN

Manuel Jean is an accountant who works at the School of Hope as an intern, being paid a stipend that is probably sufficient only to cover his room and board. His ultimate goal is to become a CPA.

Manuel grew up in Gonaives, where at age 22, he was still struggling to complete his last year of high school. His parents were unable to help. His mother had suffered a stroke and was paralyzed and bedridden. His father was next to unemployed—he worked as a street merchant, where, if he was able to sell $50 in merchandise in a day, his profit was about $5. His place of business was on the street in front of the family home.

TeacHaiti sponsors students in private schools in Gonaives and Manuel's parents had heard of the program and contacted Miquette about the need for a scholarship for Manuel to complete high school. An interview was conducted in Gonaives. Miquette reviewed the student's grades and was impressed with his intelligence and ambition. He told her "You will not be disappointed if you give me a scholarship. I will work very hard."

The scholarship was awarded and Manuel did work hard. In finishing high school he had a solid math background, but no business courses like book-keeping, accounting, computers or keyboarding.

Upon graduation, Manuel moved to Port au Prince in 2009 to enter Inuqua University under a TeacHaiti scholarship where he spent four years as a full-time student, graduating in 2013. But the goal of becoming a CPA was still a long ways away—and expensive. His internship with TeacHaiti will last a year and will enable him to move forward toward his goal which will require further studies and tests. TeacHaiti may be able to help him with some of the expenses of achieving this additional goal.

FORMER STUDENT MARIO HENRY

Mario Henry, a handsome young Haitian man is a third year university student studying economics. He met Miquette just after the earthquake when he was acting as an interpreter and translator for medical teams Miquette was assisting. Since then he has had financial assistance from TeacHaiti to enable him to continue with his education. The assistance comes in the form of a check directly from a supporter—sent to TeacHaiti, then delivered to Mario. TeacHaiti has also provided some books for Mario.

Henry has visited the School of Hope and has been impressed with what he has seen. He says education has been a luxury in Haiti, available to the very few. The kids without money or backing don't go and they are educated on the streets. There they learn violence and theft. He says education is the key for lifting up Haiti—the key to opening the gates of opportunity.

God Will Help You Write This Book

Then Henry added a personal note of his own to the interviewer: "You are doing something very important and God will help you write this book."

CHAPTER 13

A SHORT HISTORY OF HAITI

*"Those who fail to learn from history
are doomed to repeat it."*

—Winston Churchill

In order to appreciate the poverty, illiteracy and desperate need for education for Haitian children, it is necessary to have some grasp of how conditions in Haiti came to be. The history of Haiti is a long, sad tale of exploitation, slavery, repression, colonialism, imperialism, dictatorships, corruption, political treachery, incompetence, indifference, ignorance and disease.

Start with Columbus. When Christopher Columbus landed in the Bahamas in 1492, he made his way across the Windward Passage (between Haiti and Cuba) and became the first European to land in Haiti. Columbus noted that the natives, the Tainos, wore gold trinkets and seemed submissive enough to be submitted to slavery.

Columbus named the mountainous island Espanola (Hispaniola) in honor of his Spanish patrons. Present day Haiti occupies the western third of Hispaniola and the remainder is the Dominican Republic.

The native Tainos numbered about 500,000. They had an elaborate social structure organized around local chiefs, and yes—they did have some gold.

They were not as highly civilized as the Aztecs of Mexico or the Incas of the Andes, but they were getting along just fine.

Of course Columbus and the Spanish colonists who followed didn't come to settle and become farmers, they were conquistadors with ambitions to conquer the tribes, kill their leaders, enslave the natives and quickly relieve them of their gold and spices.

Within two generations, the Tainos were gone. Thousands had been killed by overwork and indifference to their suffering. Thousands died as a result of European diseases for which they had no immunity, their gold was taken and their civilization wiped out. Then get-rich-quick Spaniards moved on to the more promising riches of Mexico and Peru. Thanks Columbus.

Spanish influence diminished and eventually the French took over. They came as pirates, but eventually stayed to profit from the crops of the fertile island with the tropical climate: cotton, indigo, coffee and sugarcane. Sugar was the oil of the eighteenth century. But the French needed settlers to exploit these natural resources and no Frenchman with a job and making a living was motivated to move to the new world. Only the penniless were interested, but they had no means to buy a ticket to the new world. So French colonial authorities devised a system where free passage to the colonies was provided in exchange for a three year period of voluntary servitude.

The system was hardly ideal. France took advantage of the opportunity to clean up the streets of Paris by rounding up criminals, orphans and prostitutes and sending them over. Also, sailors in French ports discovered they had signed on while drunk. Defrocked priests and other "undesirable" elements of French society also found their way to Hispaniola, now named Saint Dominique. Even after the better elements of French society started arriving, the colony had acquired the reputation of being an unruly collection of settlers.

The economy grew, but coffee and sugar cane were labor intensive crops, hard labor, and more hands, many more hands, were needed. Many of the indentured European laborers were unable to stand up to the demands of the hard work and the tropical heat and they died by the thousands. The Spanish had brought over a few African slaves when the native Indians, the Tainos, were dying. The French decided that slavery was the answer to their labor shortage, so by 1790, at the height of Saint Dominique's prosperity, the total slave population was 500,000. But the hard work for the sugar plantations killed thousands of slaves as well. No problem—more were imported.

The slaves were "protected" by provisions of the French 1685 Code Noir (Black Code), but the law was largely ignored in the colonies. For example, an army officer who wrote about his visit to Saint Dominique said he was a dinner guest at the home of a white settler. When a slave/servant brought an over-cooked dish, she was thrown into the oven and roasted.

Among other slave societies, Haiti was known as one of the cruelest. Though torture and capital punishment were illegal under the Black Code, cruelty, even sadism were seen as the only way to control slaves. Mutilation and flogging were common. But disregard for the law has been characteristic in Haitian society, even to the present day.

American slave owners intimidated their slaves by threatening to sell them off to serve in Saint Dominique. Slave owners were outnumbered by slaves 50 or even 100 to one, so the owners had to resort to extreme measures to control the slaves. Conditions were brutal. Intense heat, tropical diseases, hard labor, insufficient food and mistreatment killed five to six percent of the slave population every year.

Most of the slaves submitted, but gradually resistance developed. Some simply ran away in spite of a police network organized to prevent slave flight. A few escaped the island entirely, while others formed small communities in the mountains. In 1702, the French sent an expedition to dislodge a community that had formed near the Haitian—Dominican border. The effort failed. For years afterward, these escaped slaves engaged in guerrilla raids on plantations and the French chased them. Finally, in 1785, the French and their Spanish neighbors gave up. They signed a treaty giving the former slaves their independence in exchange for a cease fire—no more raids on plantations.

But these former slaves, living in the mountains, called Maroons, by no means ended the slave economy. The vast majority of the slaves remained laborers on the plains.

The French slave economy created a hybrid culture. For example, the Creole language developed as a combination of French and words of African origin with grammar twisted beyond recognition. Also, the slaves from Africa brought their own gods, but were converted to Catholicism by French priests, nevertheless retaining some of their own traditions and superstitions. The result was Voodoo, a combination of the worship of ancestors, natural forces, witchcraft, black magic, evil spells and Christianity. Traces of Voodoo continue in Haiti to the present day.

In France, the French Revolution was taking place during the last decade of the 1700s. Ninety percent of the population of France was the underclass, living beneath the royalty (King Louis XVI) and the aristocrats, and they had had enough. It was time for throwing off the old order. The rallying cry of "Liberty, Equality, Fraternity" had a ring that carried over the Atlantic to the colonies, especially to the slaves of Saint Dominique (not yet Haiti).

The French Declaration of the Rights of Man and of the Citizen stated that "All men are created free and equal." The pot was stirring and the slaves decided it was time to act. They gathered in Bois Caiman while Cecile Fatiman, a female Voodoo priest and a mulatto slave of mixed Corsican and African origin performed a secret late night ceremony involving the slitting of the throat of a black pig, declaring it was slavery and white slave owners. To seal the oath, the participants drank the warm blood of the sacrificial pig then returned to their plantations. The following night the Slave Revolt of 1791-1792 had begun. The objective: freedom for the slaves. But some of the leaders, dressing themselves in royalist garb, wanted more—their own monarchy—and they negotiated a peaceful settlement with white plantation owners that left a form of slavery intact. The struggle was not over.

Finally, by 1798, a former slave, Toussaint Louverture, became the father of his country. But, like George Washington, he had slaves of his own. Educated and ambitious, by 1801 Louverture had maneuvered a constitution that made him governor general for life and the right to name his successor. This pattern was repeated many times in Haiti's history as you will see.

Louverture's economic plan was for the division of land into small scale subsistence lots, the dream of former slaves, but it was not feasible. Instead, sugar and coffee exports were required to pay the state's (and Louverture's) coffers, pay the army, buy weapons and generally to return the colony back to the economic strength it enjoyed before the revolution. The crops, especially sugar, could only be produced on large, heavily capitalized tracts. Former slaves now called cultivateurs, resumed their labors in the boiling sun. These cultivateurs were not considered slaves, as they did receive one fourth of the crop, but they were pushed hard and treated harshly. Protesters were executed.

But, some slave trade still continued and Lourverture maintained a friendly relationship with France, not necessarily consistent with individual freedom or national independence for Haiti. He was, in essence, a profitable large plantation owner with near-slaves of his own, ruling his country more like a dictator than a president.

But Napoleon Bonaparte, now ruling France, wanted France's profitable colony back, which meant the return of slavery. The French captured Lourverture and sent him into exile in a cold prison cell in the mountains of France. He died in 1803.

French soldiers in Haiti, trying to regain the colony, died in droves of yellow fever as did their commander, General Leclarc. But the French persisted: mass drownings, burning, crucifixion, rape, torture and even slave-hunting dogs were engaged to regain control. The French eventually decided that nothing short of extermination of the former slaves would keep Saint Dominique in French hands. The former slaves had tasted freedom and they had learned how to fight to preserve it. Ultimately, the French, also at war with the British, decided to give up on the island and snuck out. Finally, Haiti was an independent republic led by former slaves.

This Haitian Revolution was probably the greatest hour in Haiti's history. Haiti has never been as rich as it was in 1788 before the slave revolt. It has never been as powerful as it was from 1793-1803 when it defeated the European colonial powers, and never so inspiring as it was in 1804 when it proclaimed its independence and earned freedom for its people. This was the only time in world history that a slave revolt had ended successfully.

The road leads steadily downward from that 1804 high point. From that date until the election of the current President, Michel Martelly, in May of 2011, the country has had 56 heads of state and six "provisional" or "acting presidents." Thirty were in office less than one year with 10 of them serving less than two months (one of these only three days—Hererd Abraham was

Acting President from March 10, 1990 to March 13, 1990). If this suggests lack of stability, there is more. Of these 62 heads of state, one died of suicide, one was executed, two were assassinated and 23 were overthrown. Only 10 served full terms, but four of those were during years of U.S. occupation (1915-1934) which will be described below.

Just a few weeks after the French troops left Saint Dominique, victorious black and mulatto officers assembled to proclaim independence. A time to celebrate, yes, but also a time for revenge. Thousands of former slaves had died in the previous 13 years of fighting, many by torture and mass executions. Everything about the French was hated, so even the country's name, Saint Dominique, was erased and the original Taino name, Haiti, was adopted. As far as the new self-government was concerned, what goes around comes around, so what followed was a revenge-filled, savage program of rounding up French soldiers, planters and merchants, men, women and children and the remainder of the white population, who were massacred.

Revenge was realized, but at what price? As reported by Philippi Girard in *Haiti*:

> The 1804 massacre now occupied a prominent spot in the annals of human cruelty, and from being morally repugnant, the massacre immediately put the young Haitian republic on an ill-fated course. For all their faults, Saint-Dominique's whites had been the most educated faction in the colony. White planters organized labor on the plantations. White engineers designed irrigation projects. White bureaucrats and lawyers administered the colony. White officers manned the top echelons of the army. Even Louverture's secretaries were white. In one blind act of revenge, Dessalines (the first ruler, who had declared himself Governor-General, the Emperor of Haiti, lynched two years later by his own officers) wiped out his country's cadres. For decades thereafter, the vast

majority of Haiti's population (Dessalines included) remained illiterate and unskilled, substantially hindering Haitian economic development. Securing one's freedom in an orgy of white blood also set a violent tone for future political discourse. Following Dessalines' example, ambitious generals gained, kept, and then lost power through violent means. Only five of the thirty-four founding fathers who now gathered at Gonaives would die of natural causes. Dessalines would not be one of them.

The assassination of Dessalines occurred because the lives of former slaves and army officers had changed little and they were still under the whip. Dessalines was a dictator. What followed was more fighting, a civil war with no clear winner. The result was a divided Haiti under two rulers, Christophe in the north and Petion in the south, and two separate economic systems. In the north were large plantations with peasant labor working long, hard hours for the government. Wages were one-fourth of the crop. Profits from sugar exports funded an extensive police and state apparatus. Soldiers and spies were everywhere. In addition, Christophe built a network of massive fortresses and mansions for himself. Christophe, a former cook, had himself crowned Henri I, King of Haiti. In the south, under Petion, discipline was more lenient, but still dictatorial. The economy in the south was the carving out of plantations and dividing them among soldiers. Sugar production didn't work in small gardens, so the workers cultivated coffee, but the result was low profits. Phillipe Gerard summarized the differences between north and south:

> Northerners were working against their will and making a bit of money. Southerners were free and poor. Had the country joined the industrial revolution, gathering steam in Europe and America at that time, and pursued industrial opportunities rather than relying primarily on agriculture, Haiti would probably not be the poor country that it is today.

The dictators of Haiti remained apprehensive about the possibility that France would attempt to regain their colony. Huge expenditures were made for fortresses and other questionable projects. They were a serious financial drain on the young republic and were probably meant to defend the dictators more against their own people than against the French. As it turned out, the French never attempted a comeback.

As indicated earlier, the easterly two-thirds of the Caribbean Island originally called Hispaniola was occupied by the Dominican Republic. While Haitians have whined about foreign nations attempting to make Haiti a colony, not once (1801), twice (1805), three times (1821), four times (1849), five times (1850), but six times (1855), did the Haitians invade the Dominican Republic attempting to annex the republic to turn all the Hispaniola into a Haitian empire. Only once did they succeed—in 1821, starting an occupation that lasted 23 years. The Dominicans declared their independence in 1844 and threw off Haitian rule, though the Haitians tried three more times to regain it. Finally, economic failures in Haiti forced the Haitians to abandon their dreams of control of the entire island.

One dictator after another spent public money on military excursions, royal pomp, greed, embezzlement and personal enrichment as well as power for power's sake. The first half of the 19th century was characterized by revolutions, civil wars, coups and coup attempts, bloodshed and constant turmoil. Twenty-nine of the thirty-four original signers of the declaration of independence met violent ends. Each revolution ended with millions of dollars worth of property going up in flames. This instability resulted in schools, roads, sewer systems, factories, water systems and fire-fighting systems being neglected or under-funded. Most of the leaders were interested in acquiring and holding onto power, with very few showing any inclination toward doing anything constructive with that power. Only two presidents, Fabre-Nicholas Geffrard (1859-1867) and Lysius Salamon (1879-1888) initiated infrastructure improvements. Geggrard built roads and irrigation ditches, started a steamship company and improved schools. Solamon created a national bank, paid arrears on the national debt, modernized the army, featured public education, printed Haiti's first stamps and maintained positive foreign relations. But soon after their departure (both were overthrown), their initiatives had been neglected and fallen into disrepair.

In terms of uncertain, unstable leadership, the period between 1911 and 1915 was probably the low point in Haiti's history. Jean Vilbrun Guillaume Sam was inaugurated as president of Haiti on March 4, 1915. He never was elected, but took office behind the force of mercenaries. In the previous four years, the country had five presidents before Sam. Two had died in office and three were overthrown. Sam had a hand in the revolution that preceded him. For security, he had 200 hostages from the most prominent families of Port au Prince jailed with orders to execute them if another revolution broke out.

But less than five months after he was sworn in, a small group of revolutionaries swarmed the presidential palace in Port au Prince, captured a machine gun and turned it on the guards. Sam was wounded but he escaped out the back door, so to speak, and sought asylum at the nearby resistance of the French ambassador.

The prison guards, learning that Sam had fled, carried out their previous instructions and removed the 200 hostages Sam had arrested (to guarantee his safety) just weeks before. The hostages were butchered with clubs and machetes. When the shouting was over, 167 bodies, mangled beyond recognition, lay in their own blood.

There were 167 funerals on July 28th, burying what body parts that could be assembled. The mourning relatives of the 167 families wanted revenge.

They charged the French ambassador's home pushed past the objecting ambassador and his daughter, ignoring diplomatic immunity and presidential deference, and found Sam hiding in the ambassador's bathroom. They dragged him out kicking and screaming, beating him as they went. By the time they reached the street the president was half dead. By nightfall, the crowd had finished the grisly job and nothing remained of the president but a dismembered heap of human flesh.

This was too much. Foreign diplomats in Haiti agreed that the savage prison massacre and the violation of the French ambassador's residence, followed by the hatchet murder of the president on a public street in open daylight were beyond the pale, even by Haitian standards. Haiti had become ungovernable and something had to be done—by outside forces. Haiti was a disaster: its economy was in shambles, no sugar had been exported in the previous hundred years, public infrastructures were crumbling from years of neglect, tropical diseases were rampant, no industry existed and the capital was a dump.

The U.S. Navy came ashore July, 1915, and took control. Haiti, 111 years after their 1804 Declaration of Independence, was once again a colony. The purpose was to act as a caretaker until Haiti could get on its feet again, although to the Haitians, it was an invasion, an imperialist grab of Haitian resources. However, it must be admitted that since World War I had started in 1914, the United States didn't want Haiti to be available for Germany to take over as a staging ground for an attack on the United States. Following the policy of the Monroe Doctrine, President Woodrow Wilson decided to take Haiti before somebody else did.

A U.S.-Haitian treaty in 1915 outlined the terms of the occupation. Under the treaty, the old palace guard was given mandatory retirement, thousands of weapons were confiscated and a new Haitian police force under American officers was formed. All this was to control violence. The treaty allowed a Haitian president and congress, but under close American management. Customs and treasury were regulated so that any aspiring revolutionaries were denied access to money to finance political ambitions. The U.S. also controlled public health and infrastructures under the treaty. One very effective tactic for American control of the treasury before the ratification of the treaty was to hold up paychecks of the president and congress until the treaty was ratified.

American occupation was not popular among Haitians, but it did produce results. For the first time since 1843, Haiti experienced 19 years without a revolution. Four successive Haitian presidents served full terms.

Custom fees no longer financed revolutions and private plunder; they were directed to public works. By the late 1920's, 210 bridges and 1,000 miles of all-weather roads were built. Ports were modernized and lighthouses introduced. Telephone lines were repaired. A new presidential palace was built. Irrigation canals were repaired and expanded, enabling cotton and sugar exports to resume. Air service to Miami was established. An agricultural school was opened. Running water and 11 modern hospitals were built. During that occupation, the Haitian debt to the United States was paid in full. All these projects were financed with Haitian taxes, not foreign aid.

Despite these positive achievements as a result of the American-imposed stability, the Yankee occupation left Haitians feeling humiliated—they were colonial subjects again. Haitian pride was bruised and the American presence was resented. The Americans had failed to turn Haiti into a pro-American, prosperous, reasonably democratic society. But, American ignorance and racism played a role in this antagonism. For example, William J. Braun, Woodrow Wilson's Secretary of State, was brought up to date on Haiti's national bank and geography. His reaction: "Dear me, think of it!

Niggers speaking French." The American occupation ended in 1934. The Haitian president, Sternio Vincent, elected in 1930, continued in office and served his full term which ended in 1941.

From that point, Haiti reverted to its historical pattern. Six governments came and departed in a nine month span; three men were overthrown; two elections were cancelled, and Haiti went through a one-day Civil War. Chaos and instability again plagued the nation.

"Papa Doc" Duvalier

Along came Francis Duvalier, a shy, black physician considered by one political opponent to be a "profoundly stupid little man." But he appealed to poor blacks because he related to them on a personal level as he had spent years fighting tropical diseases in rural Haiti. Duvalier, became popular and well known in the application of penicillin to yaws, a flesh eating disease like leprosy. He was affectionately called Papa Doc, was appointed minister of health and labor and got his first taste of politics. He was elected president in 1957 on the promise to promote black-nationalism, to defend the rights of women and promote Haitian sovereignty abroad.

But Duvalier's election was protested by one of his own opponents, Lous Dejoie, who organized demonstrations and a general strike to prevent Papa Doc's inauguration. The army resisted and the inauguration proceeded, but Papa Doc learned that terror, more than democratic processes, was the best method for staying in power. He sent hundreds of political opponents to jail. Later, political opponents, men and women alike, were rounded up, loaded in trucks, then dumped into a hole and covered with dirt. Papa Doc had become a ruthless dictator, maintaining authority by imprisonment, gang rape and murder. He was challenged again and again, but results were always the same—he survived by the most cruel and brutal measures, each threat giving him another excuse to continue his always swift and always savage reprisals. Not only political opponents, but their spouses, children, parents and even friends were targeted for retaliation. No one was safe. Prominent ministers were killed or exiled when they offended him. Foreign priests were executed. Even his son-in-law had to flee for his life.

Duvalier's re-election in 1961 gave him a second six year term as president, then in 1964 he was elected "President for Life" with official results showing he had received 100% of the vote.

Historians have pondered how a shy, benevolent country doctor could become a murderous tyrant. He wasn't stupid and he wasn't insane. His corruption seems to have been the mix of total power and the constant turmoil of the Haitian presidency. He carried out this cruelty through the Haitian army, 5,000 strong, which also acted as a police force and a private para-military force known as Tontons Macoutes: Papa Doc's bogeymen. The Macoutes, male and female, eventually numbered 300,000. They created fear wherever they went with their conspicuous guns, denim uniforms, dark sunglasses and red scarves. They were everywhere.

Of the many dictators in the history of Haiti, none was worse than Papa Doc. While publicly condemning foreign imperialists and touting black-nationalism, he cleverly manipulated France and the United States into providing millions in foreign aide by making strong anti-communist statements. While political murders had been standard operating procedure for previous dictators, Duvalier added excruciating torture sessions and unspeakable detention conditions.

Many journalists and historians wrote about the horrors of Papa Doc's regime. Even a novelist, Graham Green, who visited Haiti during Papa Doc's years, made an observation in his novel, *The Comedians* (1966), admittedly a work of fiction about the dictator,: "poor Haiti itself and the character of Doctor Duvalier's rule are not invented, the latter not even blackened for dramatic effect. Impossible to deepen that night." Green learned to his delight that Papa Doc had read the book and hated it.

Papa Doc ruled for 14 years and died of natural causes in 1971 at the age of 64. When he died, the Haitians were even poorer that they had been in 1957 when he was first elected.

Jean-Claude "Baby Doc" Duvalier

Before he died, Papa Doc organized a sham plebiscite appointing his son, 18 year old Jean-Claude Duvalier, president for life. The son was chubby and round faced and soon earned the nickname of Baby Doc. The young man's main interests at that time had nothing to do with politics—he preferred to spend his time with fast cars and beautiful women. It was expected that he wouldn't last one year in office.

Baby Doc's speeches, written by speech writers and delivered in a droning voice, promised political liberalization and economic development. The U.S. was relieved that the brutal Papa Doc was no longer in power and became more generous in foreign aid with his son at the reins. In the last years under Papa Doc, U.S. aid averaged $3.8 million a year. Believing that Baby Doc would abandon his father's repressive policies, America was sending $35.5 million by 1975. But, millions of dollars were lost through corruption. Baby Doc demonstrated a greed that was never part of his father's style.

Under Baby Doc, a tourist industry developed because Haiti soon adopted a "quicky divorce" law and grew a sex industry. In addition, an assembly sector came about, employing some 60,000 Haitians making everything from t-shirts, electrical products and baseballs. At one point all the baseballs in the U.S. major leagues were sewn in Haiti.

By the late 1970's, Haiti's economy was virtually dependent on foreign aid which provided approximately 70% of the national revenue. Baby Doc shrewdly realized that Haiti's poverty could be its chief source of income. He used starving children to generate aid, then skimmed funds to private foreign bank accounts for his own use while keeping the Haitian people at a pitiful level of misery. It worked because of genuine foreign sympathy and anti-communism due to the threat of Cuban infiltration.

Additionally, under Baby Doc, Haitian entrepreneurs developed a lucrative trade in body parts, exporting Haitian blood, plasma and cadavers to American hospitals and medical schools. At the same time, Port au Prince was becoming the brothel of the Caribbean. Tourists with a taste for sexual perversion found they could be serviced through the exploitation of Haitian children.

An over-population problem was developing and peasants were moving by the thousands from the denuded and unproductive rural areas into Port au Prince to live in the urban slums. But the jobs there were few and many Haitians headed for Miami, New York, Montreal or even Paris. Many became boat people, sailing illegally across the Strait of Florida. Earlier under Papa Doc, educated, professional upper class Haitians had flown away because of political repression, not poverty.

1980 brought more bad news. The AIDS crisis hit Haiti with devastating effect. Contamination caused the U.S. Center for Disease Control to list Haitians in the "Four H" list of at risk groups along with heroin addicts, hemophiliacs and homosexuals. As a result, would-be Haitian immigrants were denied entry to other countries and the sex tourism industry and blood plasma trade, fortunately, dried up overnight.

Three Million Dollar Wedding

In 1982 Baby Doc took a bad situation and made it worse by marrying Michele Bennett, a divorced mother of two children, known for her beauty and alleged sexual prowess. The wedding, costing $3 million, was televised to a nation living off $200 a year. The couple lived an extravagant lifestyle with a multimillion wardrobe. Embezzlement and cocaine trade provided the funds.

Baby Doc and his bride took the blinders off the eyes of Doc's most staunch supporters who now, amidst the economic hard times in Haiti, began to doubt whether their leader really cared about his people.

Deforestation of the woods of Haiti started during French colonial times. But in the mid-twentieth century, overpopulation forced the peasants to cut trees in areas previously untouched. The trees cut were chopped into short lengths and made into charcoal for cooking. Once deforested, the top soil washed away in the rains, leaving the ground hard and baked. Erosion had left the soil washed out, hard and crusty.

Things Have Got To Change Here

Eager to please his restless subjects, Baby Doc invited Pope John Paul II to Haiti in 1993 for a visit and a red carpet banquet. The Pope kissed Haiti's ground and ignored the banquet. He delivered a televised speech in Creole and told the people of Haiti "fok sa chanj"—things have got to change here. This was a direct slam on the Baby Doc regime and it never recovered. Early in 1986, the unrest was swelling and demonstrations against Duvalier spread across Haiti, were picked up by the press, and pressure intensified. Finally, in February 1986, Baby Doc and his family grabbed all the furs and jewels they could pack and fled to exile in Paris. But, of course, millions of dollars rightfully belonging to the Haitian people were safely deposited in foreign accounts under Duvalier's name. Left behind was a nation in poverty ruined by 29 years of greedy, ruthless Duvalier rule.

Papa and Baby Doc had spoken of racial pride and nationalism as they ruled. That encouraged foreign aid. Papa Doc caused a brain drain by dissolving a literacy campaign in 1969 and chasing the well trained and well educated from the country, choosing to rule over a country of poor, illiterate and submissive subjects rather than prosperous, informed and restless citizens. This was probably a deliberate strategy to avoid a struggling economic recovery, but guaranteeing continued extravagant foreign aid. By the time Baby Doc left office, Haitian diaspora, Haitian citizens living in foreign lands, topped one million. During the reign of Baby Doc, food donated by foreign countries had the unintended and unexpected result of driving down the prices of home grown products so that the peasants cut back on production. Donated clothing had the same effect. Omnipresent American advisors were blamed for the hardships and failures rather than the Duvaliers for the resulting poverty.

Jean-Bertrand Aristide

On September 11, 1988, a priest named Jean-Bertrand Aristide prepared to deliver a sermon in his church in one of Port au Prince's poorest slums. As he spoke, a group of hit men, armed with guns and machetes plunged into the church and began shooting and hacking off limbs. Before it was over 13 parishioners were dead and many more wounded. The killers set the church on fire and ran. But Aristide, one of the intended targets, escaped into a nearby building. Many believed his escape proved that God was on his side.

Aristide was poor but well educated. As a young priest, he was noted to be bright and promising and his education was financed by a Silesian priest named Gabriel Desir. Aristide traveled to Israel, Greece and Canada earning a master's degree in psychology and a PhD in theology. In addition to his native French and Creole, he learned some Spanish, Hebrew, Greek and English.

Several short term presidents had come and gone after Baby Doc left. Aristide was not in politics at this time, studying abroad. But when he returned to Haiti he got a poor parish in Port au Prince, the capital. His preaching was cleverly directed at the remaining vestiges of the Duvalier years.

Even after Baby Doc rushed to exile, many of his supporters, including his death squad, the Macoutes, still worked to prevent meaningful change to the country's power structure. But it was time for a change. Along came Aristide known as a radio preacher who had dared speak against Baby Doc before 1986. He was famous for his oratorical skills, courage and support of the poor. He delivered his sermons in a witty, lively Creole and could make his listeners both laugh and cry on cue. Always interested in politics, Aristide entered the race for the presidency in 1990. He could have been rejected by the Election Commission because the constitution required that candidates own property in Haiti; but the commission simply ignored this clause. Young, charismatic and idealistic, Aristide was a popular choice for voters who wanted a break from Haiti's history of dictatorships. In spite of American misgivings because of his leftist views, Aristide was elected. Haitians celebrated. This natural politician was educated and dedicated. Democracy at last. Someone finally to cater to the impoverished majority. Little did the people know what a roller coaster ride would follow in the ensuing decade.

Before Aristide could move into the presidential palace, Roger Lafontant, a hard-nosed Duvalier think-alike who had been minister of the interior, who had tried to run for president, but was found ineligible because of his ties to the Duvalier administration, occupied the palace and claimed that made him president. But Aristide supporters forced him out and many of those who had supported the coup were hunted down and killed. One of the favorite tortures of the day was to douse a car tire in gasoline, throw it around a victim's neck and set it on fire, this was called necklacing. This practice got its beginning during the Baby Doc years. Aristide found it a convenient device.

Aristide's initial goal was to get Haitians out of poverty. If given free reign, he probably would have duplicated Communist Cuba, but there wasn't enough substance to his government to perform such a huge task. Besides, the Soviet Union, Cuba's chief supporter, was now in financial straits itself. Such a move would have probably cut off all foreign aid from Haiti's chief supporters: France, America, Canada, the World Bank and the International-al Monetary Fund. In order to assure the world he was not a radical, Aristide reduced the size of the Haitian National Government, maintained low tariffs, and engaged in a policy of austerity. About all he did for the poor was raise the minimum wage from $3.00 to $4.80 a day. But, as a result, he was able to get foreign aid increased from $200 million in 1990-1991 to $380 million in 1991-1992.

But Aristide was a political bungler. Instead of forming a strong coalition cabinet, he appointed personal friends as ministers. Rene Preval, an agronomist and partner was appointed Prime Minister. Aristide also immediately fired all senior officers in the army, the very army that had backed him during the coup attempt. Aristide's "winner take all" attitude after winning the election directed his energies into gutting all previous centers of power and replacing powerful people with his own chosen lieutenants, even at the risk of planting the seeds of future repercussions. He also directed the arrest of former political rivals on trumped-up charges, including Lafontant, who was convicted and given a life sentence of forced labor, although the maximum under Haitian law was 15 years. Aristide was becoming a dictator.

By purging the army, Aristide created a band of enemies who were enraged at his high handed tactics and determined to overthrow him. Less than a year after his election, his presidential palace was surrounded by the army who arrested him and were determined to kill him. But, Raoul Cedras, the new army commander-in-chief, originally appointed by Baby Doc, worried that the murder of a constitutionally elected president would turn the international community against any new Haitian government, so he relented and consented to allow Aristide to flee in September, 1991, on an American plane bound for exile in Caracas, Venezuela. Aristide blamed the U.S. for the coup that threw him out even though the Americans aided in his getaway.

A bloody struggle for power followed Aristide's narrow escape. Aristide's old supporters were the chief victims and within weeks hundreds had died. Not even a shelter for homeless children, established by Aristide, was considered a safe haven. Over the following three years an estimated 3,000 were killed as a result of political payback.

Raoul Cedras

Under the rule of Cedras, women especially received brutal treatment. The poor, who were the primary supporters of Aristide, were victimized for their loyalty to the former president. Women—even more so. In 1991-1994, murder, torture and arbitrary prison time were the standard weapons of political brutality, but rape was added as an instrument of terror. Independent investigations showed that thousands of rapes, including gang rape, often in full view of family members, took place during this period. Why women? Because men, mostly unemployed, weren't tied to the home, as were women who were there raising children, and were harder to find when the steel fist came looking. The Cedras thugs were even more brutal than Baby Doc, (Cedras' mentor), had been.

Meanwhile, the crafty exile, Jean-Bertrand Aristide, had moved to the posh Washington D.C. neighborhood of Georgetown in 1992 and polished his image as a saintly priest of the poor and friend of America, speaking of "justice and reconciliation." He urged the United States to welcome the boat people, but the American policy of forced repatriation commenced under George H. W. Bush, was not reversed when Bill Clinton was elected in 1992.

Clinton favored a peaceful return of Aristide to Haiti as president by way of an agreement with Cedras for dropping the embargo and forgiving him his brutal trespasses. But Cedras was steadfast in resisting peaceful overtures. Clinton was on the verge of invading Haiti, but Cedras didn't blink and the idea was scrapped.

The 1991 Cedras coup created a surge of boat people attempting to leave Haiti. The Haitian government claimed there was no reason for an exodus as there were no human rights violations. One boat capsized at sea and all aboard drowned. Others who reached Florida were sent back. The entire story of the boat people became a complicated issue of immigration policy, public relations and an embarrassing moral position for the United States in dealing with these poor, unwanted refugees. Some who landed in Cuba were more fortunate as many were legally admitted. Why were Haitians bailing out? The brutal rule of the army under Raoul Cedras was one very good reason, and the declining economy, with sharp reductions in foreign aid, was another. After the Cedras coup, the organization of American States in 1991, the United States and the United Nations in 1993, imposed trade embargoes which banned the sale of oil to Haiti. The purpose of the embargo was to cripple the Cedras regime and punish his well-to-do supporters. This embargo was encouraged by the exiled Aristide. It didn't work. Cedras didn't buckle and the well-to-do could afford the resulting increased costs. But the poor couldn't. They were punished severely by the policy. The embargo and the concurrent decline in foreign aid crushed the already weak Haitian economy. The poor were starving. A Harvard study in 1994 showed that 1000 Haitian children died each month as a result of food shortages.

Poverty, starvation and brutality weren't the only disastrous results of the Papa Doc, Baby Doc, and Cedras' administrations. The greatest long-term loss was the loss of capable people. Papa Doc's war on educated Haitians sent countless doctors and teachers into exile. Ultimately, there were more Haitian surgeons in Montreal than in Port au Prince. The exiles sent money to their families in Haiti, but the human capital was lost. This brain-drain took Haiti's best and brightest. If some of these diaspora could have been persuaded to return with their capital skills, they would have been of immense benefit to Haiti. But the longer they remained away, the less Haitian and the more Canadian, American and French they became.

Aristide, with funds available to the President of Haiti, which he still was, continued his campaign for American assistance for his return to power. He employed powerful and expensive lobbyists to gain influence with key U.S. officials, including Clinton cabinet officers. Religious leaders and Hollywood liberals joined in the campaign. He gained support by promising to reform and downsize the Haitian government if reinstated as president. The campaign succeeded. In September, 1994, U.S. troops were sent to Haiti, and, under threat of force, an agreement was worked out with Cedras whereby he was allowed to leave the country for Panama with perks worth one million dollars. The result was to overthrow the bloody Cedras regime and replace it with a democratically elected one. In the process, both Cedras and Aristide manipulated and used the well-meaning United States.

Aristide A Second Time

Aristide arrived back in Port au Prince in October 15, 1994, to serve the remainder of his five year term which had begun in 1991. The formerly poor priest was no longer poor and he was no longer a priest. He renounced the priesthood, enjoyed an opulent lifestyle and had a mistress, a Haitian-American lawyer, Mildred Trouillot. He promised he would fight for justice, not vengeance, but before long, his minister of the interior arranged for the murder of Mirelle Doruchn-Bertin, an outspoken Cedras supporter who had sued Aristide for high treason while he was in exile. Aristide obstructed the investigation of the FBI (American troops were still in Haiti) and the crime was never prosecuted.

Aristide worked out a policy with other Latin American Nations, the United States and Western Hemisphere countries to establish free trade. This meant low priced foreign food came into the country to the great pleasure slum dwellers who had been unable to afford the high priced food that resulted from the earlier tariffs. But the downside of free trade was that agricultural producers in the Haitian countryside were devastated because they were unable to compete, especially with low price rice produced in the U.S. So the poor rice farmers fled to the big city slums looking for work, and found none.

Haiti was once again dependent on foreign aid. Aid agencies having learned from past mistakes, attempted to rechannel funds to avoid fraud and reduce dependency. One result of the continuing economic crisis in Haiti was that financial problems virtually destroyed the public school system. The only schools remaining were foreign-funded parochial schools and local private schools. For the children of the Haitian poor, there were no schools at all.

As Aristide completed his five year term, he ignored the pressing problems of his people: hunger, law and order, judicial reform, the restavek disgrace and AIDS. Instead he blamed the very countries that had returned him to power and provided financial support for the problems of Haiti.

Rene Preval

At the end of his term, Aristide was not eligible to run for reelection. The constitution required him to wait five more years. The result was that 53 year old Rene Preval was elected president and inaugurated in February 1996. This was the first time that one democratically elected followed a previous democratically elected president—one of the few peaceful transfers of power in the 20th Century.

Preval was well qualified. An agronomist by training, he promised to modernize the lagging agricultural sector that had been neglected by Aristide. When Papa Doc was running the country, Preval and his family fled to Belgium and the United States where he learned French and English to supplement his native Creole language. He was a compassionate man and when he returned to Haiti in the 1980's he assisted Aristide in running shelters for homeless children. He gained extensive government experience, having served in Aristide's prime minister in 1991.

Under Aristide, agricultural lands were owned by the state. But foreign investors and Haitian agricultural workers pushed for privatization. Preval, who was not nearly as popular with his native Haitians as Aristide, attempted to privatize, but met with resistance by the out-of-power Aristide. Rather than support his former ally, Aristide postured for a return to power. He was quoted in a French newspaper as saying that Preval was "closer to zero than mediocre."

Due to Aristide's undermining of Preval's efforts, privatization became a controversial issue and divided the Haitian Parliament. An economic crisis followed with many resignations from 1997-1999, and foreign benefactors, losing confidence in the government, cancelled or reduced pledges, the result being that foreign aid income was reduced by almost half.

The United Nations Human Development Index (HDI) includes life expectancy, literacy rates, access to health resources, national wealth and income distribution. Because of the political and economic crisis of the late 1990's, all indexes showed that Haiti was in a deep poverty that billions of dollars in foreign aid had failed to ease. Haiti's HDI was 137th worldwide in 1995 and had slumped to 150th by 1998. At that time Haitians had a life expectancy of 57 and a literacy rate below 50%. Three quarters of the Haitian population had no access to vaccines or clean drinking water. Bottom line: a full 80% of the nation lived in poverty and Haiti was, by far, the poorest nation in the Western Hemisphere.

To compound the misery, the Haitian National Police were mired in political infighting to see which party could control the police to the extent that their loyalty would prevent political rivals from taking power. The result was assassination attempts, corruption and lawlessness. In this atmosphere, the only winners were those in the drug trafficking trade. Haiti was a perfect strategic location for cocaine coming from Colombia to Florida. By 1999, 14 percent of cocaine coming into the United States came through Haiti. The complete government breakdown in Haiti was the main reason.

Aristide A Third Time

In 2001, Aristide had completed his five year waiting period and was eligible to run again for president. He ran, in an election characterized by fraud, threats, coercion and murder, and was elected again by a reported ninety two percent. But the United Nations and foreign supporters were getting frustrated by the lack of progress in Haiti and the term "Haiti fatigue" came into use, believing that Haiti had blown its chances for continued world support. The United States withdrew its humanitarian mission. One of Aristide's cabinet appointees was the minister of cooperation whose main duty was to obtain foreign aid. But the U.N. and the U.S., familiar with Aristide's duplicity, were turning deaf ears on Haitian pleas for help.

Aristide initiated a law and order policy to reduce crime. But his definition of law and order was cowboy-style justice administered by trigger-happy policemen who operated as out-of-court judges and juries. Their job was to ensure support for Aristide and as a result, there developed a culture of political murder, murder of journalists, even judges. Bribery, of course, was practiced with impunity.

By the end of 2001, Aristide was a world removed from the idealist priest with a slum parish he had been when first elected eleven years earlier. Now he was wearing custom-made suits and a presidential sash, traveling abroad with an entourage of bodyguards and hangers-on. He was feted on billboards and national TV, while completely out of touch with the impoverished Haitians who had been his original supporters. He was more concerned with preventing his overthrow than on carrying on a constructive program.

Aristide promised to build bridges, hospitals and schools in his inaugural speech. Those projects remained on the drawing boards. Instead, he was spending big money on lobbyists in Washington D.C. in attempting to bring back the old cash flow. Fruitless. But public money was spent in making the President's residence even more luxurious. As Philippe Girard expressed it:

Many a Haitian child, obliged to walk for miles in search
of potable water for her family, must have looked with envy
at the large, pool the president had built for his two daughters.

The Aristide administration was characterized by a clumsy series of blunders, scandals, incompetence and a flourishing drug trade. Haitians complained that their country was the only one with a last name, as in American broadcasts beginning "Haiti, the poorest country in the Western Hemisphere..." Transparency International conducts an annual survey of the world's most corrupt countries. Haiti appeared for the first time in the 2002 summary as eleventh. It moved up to third in 2003 behind Bangladesh and Nigeria, then to the top spot in 2004, the country's bicentennial.

Aristide blamed all of Haiti's problems on foreigners, especially the U.S.A. and France. He claimed that France owed Haiti the sum of $21 billion for events dating back to 1825 when Haiti paid France in exchange for diplomatic recognition. The amount was calculated by making extensive use of compound interest and adjustments for inflation. France immediately rejected the claim as a ridiculous joke. But Artistide didn't back down. In a bicentennial address to the Haitian people he explained that their misery was "a result of a 200 year-old conspiracy" and that the $21billion France owed could bring free schools, eliminate illiteracy, reduce the poverty rate from 56 percent to 28 percent, build ten thousand public housing units, new roads, generous welfare subsidies and around-the-clock electricity— all paid by France.

The natives were growing restless. A rebellion was developing and growing rapidly. A rebel force was surging in Northern Haiti and moving south. The rebels threatened that thousands of troops were marching to overthrow Aristide.

Aristide—Out For Good

The United States and France, as well as the Haitian people themselves, were fed up. They decided that Aristide was undemocratic and unreliable. Some labeled him as a fascist thug. American and French officials met with Aristide and informed him they would not defend him if the rebels overtook the capital and he would be wise to leave for exile while he could still get away. Aristide realized the rebels would probably kill him if they got their hands on him, so he ran for it. He left at dawn the following Sunday, February 29, 2004. Aristide had been the first Haitian president to regain office after being overthrown, now he was the first to be overthrown twice. After negotiations, U.S. troops arranged for the dictator to leave for Antiqua, then to the Central Africa Republic.

But the United States, Canada, Chile, France were not about to allow the brutal, cocaine-linked rebels to take over Haiti. They rushed troops to Port au Prince to prevent yet another disastrous government. They assisted in the formation of a provisional government led by Gerrard Latortue as prime minister. Bad choice. Latortue was unpopular and suspect as a Haitian-American puppet, and his people spent much time bickering among themselves. Haiti was ungovernable, terrorized by gangs, and law and order had largely broken down. The U. N. had sent in a peacekeeping force, but it was too small to patrol the capital effectively.

More Bad News

More bad news followed. In September, 2004, tropical storm Jeanne hit Gonaives and a flash flood leveled entire sections of the populous city. The rain eroded Haiti's hillsides washing down tons of precious topsoil. Rivers overflowed their banks and dumped six feet of muck on Gonaives. Fifteen hundred Haitians died, another thousand were missing and three hundred thousand were left homeless. Fields and orchards of Haiti's prime agricultural productive area were ruined.

What followed was injury, sickness, hunger, distress, and delay. The first emergency truck of food and medicine was not sent by the Haitian government, but by the World Food Program. But it did no good because it was hijacked at the Gonaives city limits by local warlords who looted the cargo and sold it. Other food shipments and medical relief were delayed by gangs who were stopping traffic. Meanwhile, the Haitian government, under Prime Minister Latorue, declared a state of emergency and a three day mourning period, hoping for foreign aid, but delayed in providing any direct relief, being preoccupied by political clashes in Port au Prince. Philippe Girard looked back at the first two hundred years of Haitian independence with the following observations:

> Haitian expert Robert E. Maguire has coined the expression "predatory elite" to describe the peculiar blend of gangsterism, populism and outright theft that has defined the country's political superstructure for most of its two hundred year history. As mistletoe feeds off a tree, Haitian leaders have sucked away billions of dollars of their starving countrymen's money while offering nothing of discernible value in return. The chaotic situation of post-flood Gonaives was a particularly egregious example of parasitism; but political bloodsuckers had bled Haiti white, drop by drop, for decades before. They had merely been more discreet while performing this task.

It is always difficult to understand how one can be so cruel and heartless. How can well-fed gang leaders snatch food away from hungry children after they have spent three days on a roof mourning their mother's drowning? How can a restavek owner beat up a seven-year-old child for forgetting to scrub the floor after she woke up at dawn? How can a president watch a man burn to death and then call for more grisly scenes of necklacing? How can Haiti's first lady spend millions of dollars on a fancy wardrobe when peasants take their children away from school because their precious pigs were slaughtered under the eradication program her husband approved? Such behavior betrays the most basic principles of human decency.

What is even more puzzling in Haiti's case is that several of the most rapacious leaders started their lives as ordinary, even good hearted people. Faustin was a debonair army officer before an interrupted nap turned him into a ruthless dictator and imperialist. Francois Duvalier was a doctor who saved thousands of Haitians from the crippling decays of yaws before he turned into merciless autocrat with a fondness for torture chambers. Jean-Bertrand Aristide was a kindly priest who defended orphans before he reneged on his vows of celibacy, betrayed his country, denounced his foreign allies and started ruling Haiti as if he were the godfather of one of New York's five Mafia families.

A period of instability followed the exile of Aristide. Lawlessness and gang wars in the slums were characteristic of the unpopular Latortue's ineffective administration. A string of hurricanes and tropical storms, Jeanne in September of 2004, described earlier, Dennis in July 2005 and Alpha in October 2005, combined with political infighting, kept the government from addressing the country's long term problems like education, environmental ruin, healthcare and infrastructure. The storms did generate more foreign aid, but very little of that trickled through the bureaucracy to the benefit of hurricane victims. Latortue spent huge sums on expensive overseas trips in which he lobbied for further foreign aid. Again, corruption was responsible for diverting the money from its intended use. Latortue was never forced to account for the many irregularities of his administration and when his time in office ended in the spring of 2006, he left the country and retired in Boca Raton, Florida.

The U.N. Peacekeeping Mission in Haiti (MINUSTAH) did almost nothing to bring political stability to Haiti and certainly had no hand in governing the country. Their activities were largely limited to maintaining order in downtown Port au Prince and assisting in the distribution of humanitarian aid. They were also delegated to organize democratic elections. Ten lives of U.N. peacekeepers were lost in the frustrating process. Finally, the beleaguered and heavily criticized commander of MINUSTUH shot himself in his hotel room.

Rene Preval – Things Improving

Finally, two years after Aristide's overthrow, presidential elections were held in February, 2006. The election, which, as usual, involved fraud and corruption and was won by Rene Preval, a former prime minister, friend and ally of Aristide, but mild mannered and conciliatory. Preval succeeded in reducing gang violence and kidnapping, and in the process, gaining substantial foreign aid and debt relief from the international community between 2006 and 2009.

During that 2006-2009 period, positive signs began to emerge on the bad-news island. The U.S. congress passed the Haitian Hemispheric Opportunity through the Partnership Encouragement Act (HOPE) that offered Haitian-made garments custom-free access to the United States. As a result, U.S. apparel makers like GAP, Levi Strauss and Joseph A. Bank opened assembly plants in Haiti to provide jobs for the unemployed.

As the political atmosphere stabilized, the tourism industry began a slow recovery, though the acute shortage of hotel rooms and weak infrastructure were obstacles. American Caribbean cruise ships, which were not permitted to stop in Cuba because of the U.S. embargo, began stopping at the Port of Labadie (called "Labadie, Hispaniola" in cruise brochures to avoid scaring tourists with misgivings about Haiti), producing tax income from every tourist getting off the ships as well as jobs for Haitians in the local food, handcraft and general tourism industry.

The absence of bad news coming out of Haiti during this short period of tranquility encouraged foreign commerce and the Haitian economy slowly began to improve.

But bad news struck again. First, there was a spike in world food prices that generated food riots among the Haitian poor. However, rice subsidies put in place by Preval lessened the impact of the world prices and the demonstrations quieted down. Then, there were four more hurricanes and tropical storms in 2008—Fay, Gustav, Hanna and Ike, causing 793 deaths, mudslides, and huge economic damage. Finally, there was the mother of all disasters—the epic earthquake at rush hour on January 10, 2010 which nearly leveled Port au Prince and much of southern Haiti, killing over 200,000 and wiping out the progress made in Haiti in the few previous years.

The Earthquake

*"God is our shelter and strength, always ready to help
in times of trouble. So we shall not be afraid, even if the earth
is shaken and mountains fall into the ocean depths."*

—Psalm 46: 1, 2

The quake had a magnitude of 7.0 "Why Haiti?" Hillary Clinton, U.S. Secretary of State asked. The nation was already reeling from so many other man-made and natural disasters. It wasn't the worst earthquake Haiti had experienced. On June 3, 1770, there was a quake that measured 7.7 that destroyed prisons, hospitals, churches, government buildings and homes, though only 200 people died. But the 2010 quake produced the deadliest natural disaster ever recorded in the Western Hemisphere. Two centuries of corruption and political chaos had left Haiti totally defenseless.

Port au Prince had become an urban center as a result of late 20th century migration from the countryside. Over one third of the nation's population lived in that crowded city located on a well-established fault line. Zoning wasn't a priority at that time and no attention was given to the enforcement of the few building codes that existed. Architects and engineers, many without training, had built quickly—anywhere and any way. In the first twenty-four hours after the quake at least fifty four aftershocks greater than 4.0, including five greater than 5.6 were recorded. Each time the ground shook, more buildings crumbled.

The morning after the quake the toll of human life became obvious. Bodies were everywhere—in rows piled on top of one another, hanging out of walls. On one corner, four little girls, not yet teens were lying in a row. Many children unfortunate enough to be in school that afternoon died at their desks when their fragile schools caved in on them. Hundreds of government workers died in the National Palace and the ministries. One hundred two staffers died in the collapse of the U.N. Headquarters at the Hotel Christopher—the largest single loss of life in U.N. history. There never was an official count of the earthquake deaths. The first estimate by the Haitian government was 10,000, then 50,000, 111,481, 230,000 and finally 316,000. The U.S. agency for International Development (USAID) conducted a household survey and estimated 85,000 died, while a team of U.S. academics reported that the real figure was 158,000. Of course, all were estimates because many bodies were never recovered and undoubtedly remain buried to this very day.

Where is Preval?

President Preval froze. "Where is Preval?" the stunned nation asked. Even those close to the president did not forgive him for not making a national speech, a few words of sympathy and hope, after the worst catastrophe in his country's history. He became largely unavailable. Four days later, President Obama deployed search and rescue teams, provisions for food, water and medical assistance. He announced an initial disbursement of $100 million and concluded with an announcement: "To the people of Haiti, we say clearly, and with conviction, you will not be forsaken, you will not be forgotten. In this, your hour of greatest need, America stands for you."

Aid came from all directions. John Travolta came in his private Boeing 707 packed with food. Red Cross, Oxfam, Doctors Without Borders, Islamic Relief Worldwide UK, Acupuncturists Without Borders, scores of NGOs (Non-Government Organizations), Land Rovers and military caravans came pouring into Haiti.

The first priority was to save lives. Mexico, Luxembourg and Iceland sent search and rescue teams. But there were not nearly enough. Some areas of Port au Prince received no help for five days. By then it was too late. Rescuers were too few and too late. Six U.S. teams, deployed at a cost of $49 million, rescued only 47 people. Experience showed that 95 percent of rescues took place in the first 24 hours and were achieved by neighbors and passers-by. The vast majority of survivors were carried out by Haitians saving Haitians with their bare hands. Outside search-and-rescue efforts one of the largest in history, succeeded in saving no more than 211 people. Doctors and nurses (including 350 medics from Cuba) rushed in and began to perform surgeries and amputations. Israeli army medics set up a field hospital for trauma cases. U.S. military helicopters transported the injured to ships at sea while others were treated in tents.

An initial contribution of $2.21 billion was made for emergency relief by foreign governments, about one half from the United States, with major contributions by the European Community, Canada and Brazil.

Bodies were disposed of in many ways. Some were buried, some were carted to mass graves, tiny graveyards, and some were just left in piles to be buried under a soccer field—or wherever. After three days came the smell of bodies—sour, sweet, nauseous. Face masks became common. U.S. soldiers requested Vicks Vapo Rub from home to be smeared under their noses. The Haitian government provided no formal coordination of rescue efforts. But Miquette Denie and her colleagues were laboring feverishly to send the help where it was needed most. More details of their efforts in Chapters 14, 16 and 17.

There were always some who knew how, or quickly learned how, to exploit a desperate situation. Gasoline, in short supply, was being sold for the U.S. equivalent of $12.00 a gallon.

Some free food was available on a temporary basis, but one effect of free food was to depress local food prices and to deprive income to local food vendors and farmers, damaging a market already in need of repair. The need for water always had been critical in Haiti, with only a third of the population able to draw water from private or public sources. The remainder came from wells, bottled water and cisterns. After the quake, local water had to be filtered and purified and bottled water from abroad was flown in by the millions of gallons.

It was widely expected that shortages of food, water and the threat of famine would lead to chaos, riots and looting at food and water distribution points. But it never happened and violence was rare. Distribution was not well organized or coordinated, but the process improved as the fear of panic abated. All of this was generally misreported in the international press. One headline read: "Haiti nears breaking point as aid is snarled, looters roam." But an Associated Press reporter, Jonathan Katz, who had been reporting from Haiti for two and a half years before the earthquake, reported that the expected panic and terror never took place. Just as the people of New York City came together and helped one another after the attack of September 11, 2001, the people of Haiti, bound by their mutual horror, acted as a community to give aid, assistance and comfort to one another. Most Haitians appeared to be working to restore a sense of security.

We All Have Responsibility To Look Out For People Who Can't Look Out For Themselves

Disaster relief generally falls into three stages: emergency relief provided by agencies like the Red Cross and the UN World Food Programme, military and other first responders; medium term recovery provided by development-minded agencies addressing long-term needs like temporary shelter and classrooms; then finally, governments and multilateral institutions with resources to handle rebuilding and provide long-term response.

Many were moved to do what they could. George Clooney was quoted as saying "It's a big world out here and we all have a lot of responsibility to look out for people who can't look out for themselves." Clooney organized an all-star telethon that raised $61 million for the American Red Cross, World Food Programme and other non-governmental organizations active in Haitian disaster relief.

A Tarp Is Not A Tent

Sean Penn actually came to Haiti and spent seven weeks there, doing what he could. He was concerned about the relocation of Haitians displaced by the quake. Further, he worried about conditions that made the unsettled vulnerable to diseases, particularly diphtheria and cholera. "A tarp is not a tent" he stated. The tarp structure sits on toxic dirt that could carry high numbers of life-threatening bacteria. For this reason, he strongly urged that the tent/tarp settlements be moved out into open country. Penn really dug in. He met with President Preval to urge his views. Celebrities can have great influence because people pay attention to them, and Penn was widely interviewed, including on Anderson Cooper 360. He warned that the Haitian healthcare system was horribly inadequate and that unless something changed drastically, people would die in large numbers. He was also called to testify before the U.S. Senate Foreign Relations Committee in Washington, warning about a possible diphtheria epidemic. Diphtheria turned out not to be a problem, but cholera struck. Eventually, Penn was recognized for his efforts (including bringing millions of his own dollars and his own private organization, the Jenkin-Penn Haitian Relief Organization) for rescue and resettlement efforts. Six months after the quake, he, among others, including former President Bill Clinton, were given a National Order of Honor and Merit Medal by President Preval. In January of 2012, Penn was named "Ambassador-at-large of the Republic of Haiti" by its newest president, Michel Martelly.

What was needed more than anything was shelter for those whose homes had been destroyed. Tent cities sprang up overnight, one of the largest formed on a nine-hole golf course near a paratrooper food and water distribution point. Since food and water did not reach the old neighborhoods, settlement camps clustered around distribution points. But before long, a hard rain fell on the golf course, collapsing the tents and tarps and causing latrines to overflow. Over 600,000 people moved out of Port au Prince into the countryside with some moving to the undeveloped land between the capital city and the Dominican border.

Thinking Outside the Tent

The tents didn't come from the helpless Haiti government, they came from international donors. But they weren't really tents. American experience in other disaster relief venues had taught that tents were too expensive, bulky, their shape took up too much space, they were poorly designed, and lacked waterproofing. It was determined that overall, tarps were the most practical and useful. This was referred to as "thinking outside the tent." Obviously, neither tents nor tarps provided adequate shelter.

The plan was that every family in the quake zone would get a tarp. Then later, before the hurricane season, 125,000 temporary houses, called t-shelters were built made of plywood, particle board, tarp walls and metal roofs, generally of 193 square feet (under 14'x14') or less. Then finally, permanent housing, if land could be found for construction. But there wasn't enough money or enough land to carry out the permanent housing plan.

Operation Unified Response was the U.S. military's name for the six month immediate-relief phase. During those six months 2.6 million bottles of water, more than 4.9 million meals and 17 million pounds of bulk food were distributed to 3 million people. The military assisted in the distribution of plastic tarps to 1.1 million people, cleared 80 blocks of rubble, assessed the safety of 40,000 buildings, dug trenches to deter floods in nine camps, and treated 9,758 patients.

The Nuclear Solution

Even before the earthquake there were discussions outside the country of how to "fix Haiti." It was agreed there were two options. The first was for the western powers to rebuild the country one step at a time: roads,

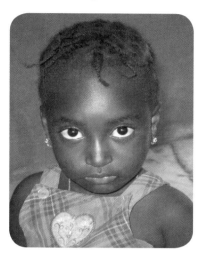

Above: The eyes of Haiti's future are upon you. **Right, Bottom Right and Bottom Left:** Will the school doors be opened for these boys?

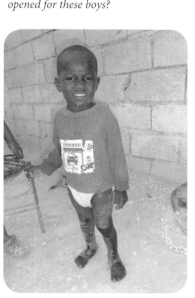

ST. MICHEL

Above: Road to St. Michel
Below: St. Michel city limits

Above: TeacHaiti signs
Left: Proud report card
Below: Classroom in St. Michel

Right: *Front door – School of Hope,* **Below Left:** *Lunch at school,* **Bottom Left:** *Flag raising,* **Below Right:** *Jewelry made by the students from recycled paper products*

Far Left:
100,000 jobs in Haiti, **Left:** *Boy in front of TeacHaiti sign,* **Below:** *Home of student, next door to School of Hope,* **Bottom:** *Beginning of school day*

Top: *Minnesota winter,*
Bottom Left: *Minnesota icicles,* **Bottom Right:**
Author showing locals ice and snow of Minnesota

minnesota

Above: *Landscaping playground*
Below: *Colorful playground*

Above: Work crew 2010, **Below:** *2012 Medical work crew*

Above Left: Motorcycle with two passenger, chickens and geese, *Above Right and Below:* Tap-tap taxis

STREET SCENES

137

Real Haiti

Right: Rush hour,
Below: Long line outside the US Embassy in Haiti,
Bottom: How did they stack these tires?

Above: Sign for Flamboyant Hotel, **Right:** Paddle
Out of Poverty poster, **Below:** Ice man

after quake

Above: Shortcut to
School of Hope
Right: On the street
Below: Street vendors

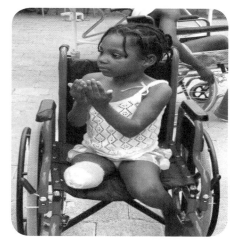

Top: TeacHaiti class, **Middle Left:** *Miquette and student,* **Middle Right:** *Child after quake, leg gone,* **Bottom:** *Orphanage children with special needs*

*Right: Children eating mush at the orphanage, **Below:** Smiling boys*

neighborhoods, agriculture, industry, security, government, etc., just like the multibillion dollar U.S. Marshall Plan to rebuild Western Europe after World War II. The second option was a sick joke: clear all the people out, drop a nuclear bomb and start over. In either case, the fix had to come from a transformative outside source.

Sending money to Haiti is not a simple matter. Foreign aid isn't just handed over to a floundering country. Much of it is directed to contractors and non-governmental organizations of the donor country in an attempt to avoid incompetence and corruption in the donor government. So most of the money is actually spent in the country of origin, not in Haiti.

The argument is made by Jonathan Katz, author of *The Big Truck That Went By* (the sound of the earthquake as it was happening), the subtitle of which is "How the world came to save Haiti and left behind a disaster," that rather than reducing direct aid to the Haitian government, it should be increased so that the government could pay salaries directly to Haitian workers, like traffic cops and customs officials, already working below the poverty line, and to step up training and monitoring. That way the money would be spent in Haiti rather than elsewhere. Under the Preval presidency, though it was clumsy and awkward, the country was enjoying relative peace and political freedom, while being popular with the poor, and had never been accused of the abuses and corruption of its predecessors. But ninety-nine percent of humanitarian funding after the earthquake had gone to the Red Cross, contractors, UN Agencies and not to the Haitian government. Preval's prime minister said: "In a lot of instances, we as a government do not receive the money. The money is going through NGOs or the institutions, but we are the ones accused of corruption for the money that we did not receive." The answer then to the question of what has Haiti done with all that money is that they never got most of it. Ironically, much of the money pledged was never paid—to anyone.

Cholera

Sean Penn had warned about Cholera, a fast moving merciless killer. But there hadn't been cholera in Haiti for at least a hundred years. As of the 2010 earthquake, not a single case of cholera had been documented in Haiti. Yet, on Sunday, October 17, 2010, Rosemond Lorime, a 21 year old, living in a mud and thatch house on Haiti's central plateau, was desperately ill. He had an intense pain in his gut with headaches, fever, diarrhea and was vomiting. His family had scratched up what money they could raise and hauled him to a little mountain hospital on a motorcycle. Too late—he died. In the next three days forty-one more Haitian with the same symptoms had also died.

The office of Coordination of Humanitarian Affairs in Haiti sent a team of international specialists sixty miles from Port au Prince to the Saint-Marc Hospital to determine what the new disease was. The locals were scared and foreigners were terrified. Was this somehow the result of the stench of decomposition from the thousands of corpses in the streets?
By the end of that first week, scores of cases of severe diarrhea had shown up at five hospitals in the Artibonite River Valley and Central Plateau. At the end of the weekend, two hundred were dead.

Tests of samples taken to the hospitals and laboratories confirmed that the disease was indeed cholera. But how did cholera get into Haiti? Poverty doesn't cause cholera, though it spreads through contamination of food or water by human waste. The bacteria called Vibrio Cholerae can quickly lead to severe dehydration and death, but it doesn't come from nowhere. Without Vibrio Cholerae, you don't have cholera, and because Haiti had never experienced the bacteria before, the people had no immunity to it.

Early on, it was clear that the outbreak was centered along the nation's largest and important river, the Artiboniti River. Investigation uncovered a broken

PVC pipe running from latrines coming out of a UN base housing Nepalese soldiers in Haitian on relief duty. The stream from the broken pipe was carrying a foul-smelling black liquid toward the river. Tests proved that the liquid carried the Vibrio Cholare, and it had been carried over from Nepal through the Nepalese, UN emergency workers, but the UN would never admit it. Unfortunately, the UN had not screened its soldiers or followed international standards of sanitation at its UN base along the river.

The Artiboniti River had become a channel of disease. At least 1.5 million Haitians depend on the river for drinking water, cooking, washing, bathing and carrying away their waste. Over two thirds of those with cholera reported drinking untreated water from the Artiboniti before getting sick.

The family of the first victim, Rosemond Lorime, left their home and moved farther away from the UN base and the broken pipe. After they left, neighbors burned their little house to the ground. From the beginning of the epidemic, over 7,500 Haitians had been killed by cholera and at least 580,000—6 percent of the population of Haiti had contracted the disease.

Michel "Sweet Micky" Martelly – President of Haiti

Though the earthquake changed everything in Haiti, the presidential election of 2010 was still scheduled to take place on November 28th. Sitting president, Rene Preval, one of the rare democratically elected presidents in Haitian history, intended to run for another five year term. But Preval's "post-quake paralysis" was a huge problem, not only for foreign governments, but Haitian voters as well. Preval decided not to run, so his party, the United Party, nominated Jude Celestin as its candidate.

There were eighteen men and women on the initial list of candidates and Celestin was considered the frontrunner. One candidate was Wycliff Jean, born in Haiti but raised in Brooklyn. He became a musician and formed a hip-hop, soul and reggae band. He spent almost no time in Haiti, but showed Haitian pride, often with a flag on his head. He was popular in his homeland because he had struck it rich. He gradually became interested in politics. When he finally announced he was running for president, he was greeted with enthusiasm. In a country that loved its music, Wycliff connected. But his candidacy was challenged. After all, he may have been born in Haiti, but he lived in the United States. Finally, he was ruled ineligible to run for president. But young voters realized they didn't have to elect a politician—they could elect somebody who hadn't betrayed them—somebody who knew how to connect.

The preliminary ballot had nineteen candidates. From among these, the two front runners would face off in a runoff election unless one candidate received more than 50 percent of the votes on the first ballot. One of the nineteen was another musician, Michel "Sweet Micky" Martelly. Martelly was one of Haiti's great showmen who was famous and popular for his raunchy suggestive music and on-stage conduct, performing Haitian kompa music. Micky was born in Port au Prince, but spent years in Miami where he entered and dropped out of a community college. Back in Haiti he felt that his kompa music was getting dated and he needed to find something new, like hip-hop or something else. Being discouraged with what he saw going on around him in his home country, he began to make pessimistic political statements about the future while on stage. Finally, he jumped into the race. It didn't hurt that the handsome, 50 something candidate with the shaved head was a musician. The Wycliffe Jean fans finally had somewhere to go. Martelly understood that voters might trust him only because of his music. But he acquired political polish as the campaign went on.

You're Nobody Until Somebody Tries to Kill You

It is said that in Haitian politics, "you're nobody until somebody tries to kill you." Three of the Celestin convoy were killed in an assassination attempt on Celestin and two supporters of candidate Charles Henri Baker were shot dead. One Martelly worker was killed, through the campaign used bullet-proof cars. This was old time politics as usual in Haiti.

The election took place amidst confusion, allegations of fraud, voting delays, requests that the election be annulled, calls for arrest and reports of police firing tear gas.

The votes were counted and the results announced on December 7th in an atmosphere of great tension. The preliminary results had Mirlande Manigat leading with 31.37 percent, Celestin in second with 22.48 percent. Martelly was out by less than 1 percent. Martelly supporters were outraged and three days of riots followed. During that time the Preval Celestin Unity Party headquarters was burned down. On December 17th the Organization of American States announced it would form an independent team to recount the votes. The team consisted of four Americans, two French, one Canadian, one Jamaican and a Chilian IT specialist. The recount result left Manigat in first place, Martelly in second and Celestin was out.

A New Haiti Is Open For Business Now

The final faceoff election was scheduled for March 20, 2011. The two candidates couldn't have been more different. Martelly was an aggressive, boisterous showman. Manigat was a 70 year old law professor, a grandmother, professional and dignified. But their platforms were not far apart: both were conservatives, nationalistic, law-and-order advocates who would encourage foreign investments with tax breaks, allowing foreign companies to take all their profits out of Haiti—the"Haiti open for business" view. The final results were not even close: Martelly 67.5 percent and Manigat 32.5 percent. On May 15, 2011, "Sweet Micky" was sworn in as president. Former president, Bill Clinton, was present to witness the ceremony. In his acceptance speech, Martelly shouted: "This is a new Haiti! A new Haiti is open for business now."

Is there still corruption in Haiti under Martelly? Oh yes, at least a little bit. After arriving at the Toussoint International Airport in Port au Prince in March of 2013, I cleared customs and was headed out the door. But there were four uniformed (policemen? soldiers?) in position for one last check. The nearest one looked at my single bag then asked to check my passport. He looked at it and raised his eyebrows. After a split-second delay, he said in a quiet voice "Twenty bucks and you can go through." "I don't have twenty bucks" I said. After another split-second delay I just walked past him. Then I looked back and my bodyguard Jeff was just allowed to pass after coughing up five bucks. Somebody is letting that happen.

Is it a new Haiti? The folks interviewed in Haiti by the author of this book responded with cautious optimism. Martelly has started to build roads and bridges, he is talking about creating jobs and getting the economy going again, about not rebuilding the presidential residence until Haitians are out of tents and in homes. They've heard all that before, but they like Sweet Micky and this time they want to believe it.

CHAPTER 14

ADVISORS AND SUPPORTERS
IN PORT AU PRINCE

*"There is a magnet in your heart that will
attract true friends. That magnet is unselfishness,
thinking of others first; when you learn to live
for others, they will live for you."*

—*Paramahansa Yogananda*

Art McMahon is Miquette's husband. Art is a white, handsome, well built, open, friendly, regular guy. They were married on October 15, 2011. Art was employed as a full-time teacher and coach at the Quisqueya Christian School when Miquette started working there first as an occasional substitute, then on a six month assignment, January through June, 2008. The school was looking for a nurse and Miquette was hired full-time in August, 2008.

 The couple became acquainted that fall and had lunch together from time to time at noon at the school's outdoor lunch tables. According to Art, it was a low-key, platonic beginning. But Miquette really caught Art's attention in September of 2008 when both volunteered to work on a cleanup detail at a mission compound following Hurricane Hanna. The task was to clean up mud. Miquette showed up in designer jeans, all made up, hair just perfect and wearing loopy earrings. Art says

she was the first to grab a shovel and walk into the mud, laughing, encouraging and having a great time. She was a terrific worker and when the work was finished, she still looked great. This was a turning point in Art's attitude, but he was still being cautious.

Students and staff were starting to pay attention to the more frequent, but still slow-moving, lunch meetings. They received a few encouraging chocolate/vanilla cards referring to the black-white relationship. Art still considered it casual and "unofficial."

On Easter weekend in 2009, Miquette invited Art to come with Miquette's mother, Rose, and other family members to Miquette's old hometown, St. Michel, for the holiday. Walking together on the street in St. Michel, some guy asked Art if Miquette was his girlfriend. It wasn't a challenge, just a friendly question. Art explained that they were just hanging out with one another. Art says he now knows that in Haiti, there is no understanding of a slow-moving, causal getting-acquainted period. She's either your girlfriend or she's "fair game" for some other guy. The guy asked him
"Are you living together?"
"No."
"Are you living alone?"
"Yes."
"Is she living alone?"
"Yes."
So then the guy looked at Miquette and asked her, "Can I come live with you?"
At this point, Art felt he had to declare himself. He said "No—she's my girlfriend."

Some background about Art. Art grew up in Tallmadge, Ohio, a suburb of Dayton. He graduated high school at the Cuyahoga Valley Christian

Academy and earned his college degree at Asbury University in Willmore, Kentucky with majors in health and physical education. Then he earned his masters degree. After his masters, he came to Haiti to teach health and physical education and to coach the basketball team at Quisqueya Christian School for a year and a half from January, 2000 through June, 2001. Then he returned to the U.S. and for one year and taught fifth grade in Kentucky at the Lexington Christian Academy, followed by four years of teaching and coaching basketball at his old high school in Tallmadge, Ohio. Then for a year he was out of education researching companies for stock market background. Lucrative work, but not satisfying.

He always wanted to return to Haiti. He said he knows he would have regretted it if he had not returned. An opening developed at Quisqueya, he was granted a six month tentative placement in January 2008, and he's still there, back in Christian education. In August of 2013, Art was named Secondary Principal (grades 7-12) of the Quisqueya Christian School. He is still Athletic Director and, though his class schedule has been changed, he is still teaching. He says he is working at Quisqueya, as most of the staff are, not on salaries but on stipends amounting to about 40% of what they'd be earning in the U.S.

Black Don't Crack

Art brought Miquette to meet his parents in Ohio in 2009. He told them "This is an awesome woman who loves the Lord. She is a one and only who gets more and more beautiful with time." It wasn't long before they got to know her and embraced her like a daughter. Art says "They love her to death." They once asked her why, at age 34, she still doesn't have a wrinkle or show her age. Her answer was "Black don't crack."

Miquette Lost—You Do The Pushups

Miquette is not only involved in her work, but Art's work as well. During the 2011-2012 basketball season, in addition to his duties at Quisqueya, Art coached a semi-pro basketball team, LaCourone, playing in a 10 team Haitian league. Miquette came with Art to team practices and games, bringing her first aid kit along. She not only attended to the minor injuries of Art's team players, but eventually opposing players as well. LaCourone eventually played for the national title but finished second. One day after practice, Miquette went out on the basketball court to shoot baskets. She is very athletic according to Art. On a bet with one of the players, she made 8 consecutive free throws. The player who lost the bet was doing pushups. Then later, Miquette came to Art and said she'd lost the next bet and Art had to do the pushups.

Art says Miquette is always a nurse and ready to serve. Sometimes street people knock at the gate of the Quisqueya School because they need help from the neighborhood nurse because of a cut leg or some other injury. When some pedestrian gets hit by a car (this happens with some regularity where the streets are narrow and there are no sidewalks), Miquette doesn't walk by, she stays and helps. Art says she has a heart for the people of Haiti.

Art, who got his master's degree in education before moving to Haiti, has become a member of Miquette's TeacHaiti team. He misses his family in Ohio, but there is no pressure from them to return. He says the great thing about TeacHaiti, and the reason it works so well, is that it is by, with, and for Haitians. He says if Miquette died in an accident, he is confident the program would go on. "When God is behind something, it's gonna work."

Art and Miquette became parents of a baby boy, Maxwell Arthur, born on June 28, 2013.

DANIELE DESROSIER

 Daniele Desrosier is one of four members of the Haitian board of TeacHaiti. She has been on the board since 2010 when it was formed. As a board member she has assisted in preparing job descriptions, helping conduct interviews of teachers and other employees, and she volunteers in many other ways. Her former husband, Kerby Jules, is also a board member. Kerby has a degree in finance, is employed as a financial consultant and advises the board on financial matters.

After the earthquake, the board spent time with Miquette about the direction of TeacHaiti. That is when it was decided to rent a home, remodel it, hire teachers and open the School of Hope to bring in students who had been attending classes at schools that had been destroyed.

Daniele's own education and experience background is that she graduated from a private Haitian high school, has taken secretarial and accounting studies, speaks five languages and has worked as a translator. She was enrolled in the University of Cedi but withdrew when her father was unable to work and help pay tuition for her and her sisters. Now she has returned to the University where she goes every day from 5:00 – 7:30 and will complete her degree in eighteen months. She is currently employed as an office secretary at the Quisqueya Christian School where she has been for seven years.

Daniele says Miquette is determined to help poor people and cares about the kids in TeacHaiti schools. She has the perfect personality and is doing a great job. Daniel says if these kids weren't in school they would be on the street without jobs.

She says the board has asked itself the question whether the TeacHaiti program could survive if Miquette died. The board is well organized, keeps good records and she is of the opinion that the program would continue.

ROUSLYX FARDIN

 Rouslyx Fardin is a math teacher at the Quisqueya Christian School Middle School. She is a Haitian, born in the U.S. to Haitian parents. She grew up in New York and Connecticut and was educated at Florida International University, earning a degree in psychology. She is certified in special education. She is married to a Haitian who is a civil engineer employed by the U.S. Government in the AID Chemonics program on post-earthquake reconstruction projects, one at Cap Haitian and another in road construction and the relocation of government buildings. 2014 is their third year living in Haiti.

When Fardin first met Miquette she could see her passion for students. Fardin is acquainted with all School of Hope teachers. Miquette invited her to conduct some in-service tutoring before school started in September of 2012 to share her special education expertise in dealing with struggling students. The teachers have the will to cope, but lack the background. She has spoken to the teachers several times as an outside resource about best practices in dealing with children with special needs. The teachers told her on follow up visits that the children were responding to the new ideas.

I Wish I Had A Heart Like Her

Fardin says it's amazing how devoted Miquette is, not only the students, but to the kids in the neighborhoods. "I wish I had a heart like her" she says. The effects of the School of Hope go to the kids, their families and beyond the school building. She has such great passion, energy, optimism and faith, "I just love her mind." She has created an atmosphere of success for these children. She says Miquette's husband, Art McMahon, adds to the School of Hope program by bringing some of the students to the Quisqueya School for sports activities.

Fardin says the Haitian culture does not have sufficient respect for children and tends to ignore them. As a result, Haitian kids give brief answers to questions while looking down. But she tells the story of a 6 or 7 year old School of Hope girl who was waiting at Quisqueya to be picked up by her parents in October of 2012. When Ms. Fardin spoke to her the girl asked "Can I read to you?" She read a story book in French with tremendous enthusiasm, animation, expression, understanding—and confidence. She was probably a second grader and it was early in the school year. The School of Hope children have been taught to look you in the eye and answer your questions. Further, Haitian girls are generally looked upon as lesser than boys. Miquette is changing that—she is giving girls a confidence their culture is not giving.

Rouslyx Fardin is another example of Haitians returning to Haiti to work with and for Haitians.

PASCALE GIRAULT

Pascale Girault works full time at the Quisqueya Christian School, half time as a nurse and half time as a teacher of calculus and chemistry to students in grades 10-12. She is a U.S. citizen who was born in Haiti.

She was educated in Haiti through high school. Then she studied electrical engineering for two years in

Puerto Rico at the Interamerica University. She worked as a nurse at a hospital in Florida until 2011 when she was notified that she had been accepted at both the University of Cincinnati and Georgetown University in the graduate midwife program. At that point, she had a decision to make. She felt "a calling" to return to her native Haiti with her education and experience to be part of the rebuilding. So she turned down the graduate opportunities and returned. Three years later she stated she has no regrets.

She was working at the hospital in Florida when the earthquake struck. She had an uncle killed in the quake. She took a two week vacation and headed for Haiti, but it was impossible to fly to Haiti so she flew to the Dominican Republic and had to purchase land transportation to Port au Prince at $300 per person for herself and her daughter. She brought medical supplies from the hospital where she worked. She arrived two weeks after the earthquake and camped with her family in tarps and tents. She helped her widowed aunt clean up their collapsed family home.

Pascale and Miquette share the same office space at the Quisqueya School, the school health center, and have had many discussions about the TeacHaiti program. Miquette recognizes that the Haitian culture requires learning and skill for survival. It is a culture of not following rules, cutting corners and corruption. Miquette's goal is to take the disadvantaged children, children of her own background, and to teach them how to read and get along with others—how to survive. She is a Haitian who has enjoyed educational opportunities. Now she wants other Haitian children to have these same opportunities.

Pascale has gone with Miquette to meetings of teachers of TeacHaiti and has watched how Miquette operates. She feels Miquette has huge drive for TeacHaiti and shows courage and strength for the program. She goes out of the way to educate, an example being that the program has reached all the way to St. Michel, Miquette's early home town, over 150 miles away (on bumpy roads, dirt roads, over mountains and through countless streams—a five hour drive). She doesn't think the TeacHaiti program could survive without Miquette because she doesn't see anybody else with her passion and energy.

MIRNA BENECHE

Mirna Beneche is one of the Haitians who left Haiti, then returned when Haiti called her family back. Mirna has been employed by the Quisqueya Christian School for 11 years, two as a French teacher, two as an office secretary and seven as the office manager.

She grew up in Haiti and graduated from high school there. Her family moved to Jamaica where she took business courses. Then they moved to Chicago where she earned a degree at the Harry Truman College. She moved about in the United States—New York and Florida.

She met her husband, also a Haitian, in Florida. He is a civil engineer who now is a private practice in the construction business. They have three children.

Fellow workers encouraged her husband to return to Haiti. Mirna and her husband were just two of the thousands of educated and trained Haitian diaspora living outside of Haiti. Finally, after much thinking and prayer, they returned in 2001 with their children. They felt they were bringing their strength, character and determination back to their homeland. All three of their children have returned to America where they are now in college—one at the University of Massachusetts, one at Penn State and one

159

at Florida State. These children, all born in the United States, have stated their intentions to return to Haiti after they graduate.

Incidentally, Mirna feels that more and more Haitian diaspora have been returning to Haiti since the earthquake. She speaks with the ferver of a patriot, proud of her nationality and hopeful about the future of her country. "We're all working to make Haiti go forward." Mirna and her family left Haiti during the "Papa Doc" Duvalier years when many educated and talented Haitians were driven out. When they returned in 2001, the country was run down and in disorder. Now it is gradually gaining ground—definitely better than 2001. But it will take a long time to reach an acceptable level.

Mirna has known Miquette since Miquette started working at the Quisqueya School in 2008 when Miquette helped her with a broken bone in her wrist. She says Miquette is more than a patriot—because she has the dream of bringing education to all Haitians. In the United States, all children get the opportunity to succeed and Haitian children should have the same opportunity. Mirna values the TeacHaiti program and believes Miquette and TeacHaiti will make a difference—because "her heart is so good." Mirna's husband has visited the School of Hope a number of times and has taken their children there when home visiting from college. Their family members have done some volunteer work at the school.

When asked about the new Haitian president, (since May, 2012), Michel "Sweet Micky" Martelly, Mirna said he is well liked and has good intentions. He was generous to the needy and helping before he was elected president, but she worries about the influence of those around him.

The Quisqueya Christian School where she works with Miquette had a 2012-2013 enrollment of 350 students: 150 elementary, 51 middle school and 94 high school.

BELONY MICHEL

 Belony Michel is a custodian at the Quisqueya Christian School who finished the 6th grade then dropped out. He's been doing his job for 25 years and the students and teachers say he's doing it well and compliment him daily.

Belony is a widower now since his wife died of a stroke in 2002. He has five children, two in TeacHaiti schools. One is a 17 years old daughter, a ninth grader who wants to become an engineer. Her father is confident she will be. One son is living with his uncle in the Dominican Republic and finishing high school. Another has just started college, studying accounting in business school.

Michel has visited the School of Hope many times as a volunteer doing whatever is needed, usually cleaning. He is sold on the TeacHaiti program because it offers so many things offered only in schools for the children of the wealthy: lunch at noon, summer camp (available to School of Hope students, but not really a TeacHaiti program), art programs and English. He feels the school is addressing the body, soul, spirit and mind of each child. Being taught by qualified teachers, he feels that shy children are gaining confidence and are no longer afraid. He says the only thing he will be able to leave his children will be their education, and with that they'll be able to get jobs and take care of themselves. He is acquainted with Miquette and feels she is an excellent person to direct the TeacHaiti program. She has a good spirit, a willing heart and likes to help people.

Understanding the purpose of the interview, Mr. Michel wanted to add some personal comments. He said to thank everyone involved in TeacHaiti. He says the program gives hope—hope for parents and hope for children. He sent greetings to all supporters—teachers and children—and said he was praying for the good health for TeacHaiti board members and supporters.

Post Quake Caution

Going from one interview to another on the Quisqueya campus, we encountered a teacher there whose name we got wrong, but we need to tell you what he said anyway. He told us he has six children. They are enrolled in three separate Port au Prince Schools in case one of the schools collapses in another earthquake.

VALENTINE VILCIN

Valentine Vilcin is a good example of what TeacHaiti is doing and can do for the young people of Haiti. Valentine was a 19 year old 11th grade student in a school where TeacHaiti children were attending under scholarships. Her fees were being paid by her mother. But it reached a point that mother couldn't come up with the tuition when it was due. The director of the school told Valentine she was going to be taken out of school for non-payment of fees, but that maybe there was a person who could help. Then she was introduced to Miquette for the first time. Miquette talked to her and said maybe TeacHaiti could help. TeacHaiti paid tuition for the remainder of Valentine's high school. She must have been a good student because Miquette selected two high school students to come to the School of Hope to help with classes and Valentine was one of them. When she graduated from high school, Miquette said they could help her with university expenses if she could pass the entrance exam. She passed and TeacHaiti helped.

Valentine attended Cedi University for four months after her high school graduation studying marketing. But the school collapsed in the earthquake and she never finished. When the university collapsed, Valentine studied business management by correspondence for a year. She is continuing to do this while she works and will be finished in one more year.

After the earthquake, Miquette came to her rescue. She called Valentine and arranged for her to get a one-month temporary job at the Quisqueya Christian School in the food service. Then in August, 2010 Miquette called her again and helped her get the full-time job she has now: Food Service Supervisor. In this position she is manager of the cafeteria, directing eight other employees, planning the menu, ordering, preparing and serving noon lunch for the students and faculty.

Valentine loves children and loves the work at the Quisqueya School. She would like to pursue a business management degree and get a better job at Quisqueya. She now speaks Creole and French, but is learning more and more English working at Quisqueya. Her interview was conducted in English by her and a language interpreter.

25 year old Valentine knows the value of education by what it has done for her and her family. She has one brother in the 11th grade at age 19 who has ambitions of a diplomatic career. One brother, age 22, a dropout, has no job and simply lives at home with their mother. Her older brother, age 27, didn't finish school, but learned to read and write and has a good job as a security person.

Valentine says Miquette is like a mother to her—a good person for her and everyone she meets. She says Miquette "really, really" cares for her. She can talk to Miquette about anything—job, dating, social problems and happiness.

Valentine has observed the restavek problem. She says it is widespread in Port au Prince, but not out in the countryside. Young girls who have not had the opportunity to learn to read and write came into the city to work without pay. They serve everybody in the family and do the most menial of tasks. Many get pregnant early. She knows that children being educated through the TeacHaiti program will end up with real jobs and will not become restaveks.

BEN AND KATIE KILPATRICK

 Ben and Katie Kilpatrick moved to Port au Prince from their home in Dallas, Texas two weeks before the January 10th earthquake to teach at the Quisqueya Christian School where Miquette was the school nurse and biology teacher.

Katie's first memory of Miquette was on the night of the earthquake. It was after dark and a five year old boy was on the street, bleeding out of his eyes, his head swollen and he had broken bones in his legs. Katie was holding a lantern for Miquette, the nurse, who was treating the boy. The boy was hysterical and his family was gathered around him. Katie thought he would die. Miquette was wrapping his broken femur. The streets were crowded. There was noise all around and the scene was chaotic. Katie was impressed by Miquette's poise and medical skill. Just before she treated the boy, Miquette had attended to an injured man on the sidewalk, Katie holding the camping lantern. The man died.

The next morning, first thing, Miquette was called to the soccer field of the Quisqueya Christian School, across the street from Miquette's and the Kilpatrick apartments (owned by the Quisqueya School) where another boy without obvious injuries had died. It fell to Miquette to explain to the boy's family gathered around him.

One of the first children attended to was "Queency," a boy with head injuries and broken bones. He was expected to die. He is now a student at the School of Hope and is so energetic he requires special attention.

Katie's husband, Ben, had met Miquette just before the earthquake and had been impressed by her work ethic.

The Kilpatricks came to Haiti looking for positions in a Christian school. Ben had been a corporate recruiter for a Dallas business firm and Katie had been a fundraiser for a Christian Ministry for children and wanted some hands-on experience. Both were dissatisfied with their American jobs and decided they wanted to do overseas mission work without fundraising duties.

Katie has a degree in religion from Baylor University in Waco, Texas and Ben has a degree in history and psychology from Texas Tech. They found the Quisqueya Christian School on-line and Katie was hired as an English teacher and Ben to teach history (World History, American History and Haitian History), psychology and to work as an assistant basketball coach.

The Quisqueya Christian School, where Miquette and the Kilpatricks work, should not be confused with the TeacHaiti School of Hope. Quisqueya consists of approximately 20% children of missionaries and 80% Haitian children. But the Haitian children aren't from poor families, they're from the "business class" or upper middle class who can afford to pay the tuition for their own children. The teachers at Quisqueya are not paid salaries, they get stipends. They're mostly young, committed and idealistic Christians.

During the time immediately following the earthquake, the Kilpatricks were in fear of riots and lawlessness and asked themselves whether they should return to Texas. But there was so much to do they realized they were needed in Haiti. They were not acquainted with any earthquake victims, so they were able to pitch in without personal mourning. They were also bolstered by observing Miquette's courage as she made hundreds of phone calls checking on the safety of TeacHaiti students and their families. They observed that some TeacHaiti money was used for short-term relief.

Ben and Katie become strong supporters of the TeacHaiti program. During the summers of 2011 and 2012, Miquette returned to Dallas with them where Vacation Bible School and fundraising banquets were held and $8,000 was raised in 2011 and $10,000 in 2012 for TeacHaiti. Some of the Bible School classes had projects to raise $350 to provide tuition, hot lunch, textbooks, and shoes for a single Haitian child. In addition, Katie's mom has come to Haiti, visited the School of Hope and now sponsors a child. These folks believe in the concept of TeacHaiti because it is a program conceptualized and run by Haitians for Haitians. They love Miquette because she understands the Haitian culture and is a role model for these children. They feel that too few Haitian women have provided this focus on education.

Ben and Katie both feel that coming to Haiti was the best decision they ever made. They have both been inspired to be teachers. But now they want to start a family and need genuine income so they will be returning to Texas and continuing their support from there.

JULIE WHITE

While visiting with friends and co-workers of Miquette and Art in Port au Prince, one friend, Julie White, presented me an unsolicited handwritten testimony:

> The ministry of TeacHaiti has touched the hearts and changed
> the lives of countless children and families of Haiti. With
> Miquette's unique background and upbringing, God has enabled

her to spearhead, lead and organize schools, outreaches, feeding programs, sponsorships, and the bringing of hope, vision and future to Haitian people.

A Dog Named Quaker

At the same time, I met Julie's daughter, Abby, about 11 years old. She had two dogs and I asked what their names were. They were Skippy and Quaker. "Do you want to know how Quaker got her name?" she asked me. "Sure." "The puppy was born two weeks after the earthquake and I named her Quaker."

OSMA JOSEPH

Osma Joseph is a small, dignified, humble, quiet, middle aged gentleman who was Miquette's sixth grade teacher when she came to school in Port au Prince.

Miquette requested that we interview Mr. Joseph because she remembers him as a dedicated teacher who really cared about all his students. He taught in the afternoon and often stayed late to answer all the questions his students had. She said he wasn't an easy teacher, but he was fair.

In response, Mr. Joseph said that many of his students, now doctors, lawyers, engineers and teachers, have complimented him with comments like "you taught me about life."

Mr. Joseph started teaching directly after he completed high school. He didn't have the money to attend a university, but he loved children and loved teaching. Later, after he started teaching, he earned a four year degree and a teaching certificate. He has been teaching 35 years now and still teaches 6th grade.

Joseph remembers Miquette as a sixth grader who was very determined, always did her homework, knew her lessons and was very respectful. She was smart, open and asked a lot of questions. He says she has changed very little to the present day.

Sixth grade is a very important grade in Haiti because following sixth grade, all students are required to take a national test, mostly in French, to be able to go onto the next grade. It was no surprise to Joseph that Miquette passed the test.

Mr. Joseph says his family understands the importance of education. He has five children. Three are nurses, one is in engineering school and one is an engineer. As for the teaching profession, he says teaching is a "gift you are giving," a very important gift for students, but that teachers are not well paid, not as greatly respected as they ought to be, and certainly not "big shots" in Haitian society. But all the big shots started out in a teacher's classroom. Very few ever express any appreciation for the gift they've been given.

The interview was conducted in the kitchen at the Rose and Cleuis Denie home, a tiny room with a refrigerator and hot plate in view. The overhead light kept going off and on.

Mr. Joseph commented that the School of Hope is a fine school in a neighborhood that really needs it. He pointed out that English is not taught in the school where he teaches, but that it is taught in the "wealthy" schools in Haiti, but few of the "poor" ones. He says being the bilingual school that the School of Hope is, is a major strength.

Mr. Joseph was not physically harmed in the 2010 earthquake, but his house was totally destroyed. He had no insurance to cover the loss. There is earthquake insurance in Haiti, but almost nobody had it because none could afford it. He has another home under construction now and he has just moved in though construction was not complete as of March, 2013.

He lived in a tent city for almost three years. Tent city living did not depress him, but it frustrated him greatly because of the loss of even minimum lifestyle standards and the stigma—the shame of living in a makeshift cluster. He said his children who were in college at the time didn't bring their college friends home to the tent city because they were embarrassed.

He said there were more deaths due to the earthquake then reported. Many collapsed buildings were still down in 2013 and many people have not been accounted for. Many families are still in denial and still waiting for the return of missing relatives.

He said that many of the people who were physically disabled, and even some who were not impaired in the earthquake, have been mentally disabled. They have dreams about the earthquake. Remember, there were many aftershocks and each time folks thought they were in another earthquake. Many still have nightmares in anticipation of the next earthquake. (Miquette still has bad dreams about the quake).
Joseph was deeply disappointed by the response of the president, Rene Preval, when the earthquake happened. He stayed away and was nowhere to be seen. Joseph greatly prefers the attitude of the current president, Michel Martelly, who he says people love because he's a people person.

NADEGE CHARLES – *Summa Cum Laude*

In the December 2011 TeacHaiti Newsletter, Miquette told the following story about Nadege Charles who was determined to become a nurse and persistent in seeking assistance:

> In 2007, a young woman named Nadege Charles came to me and asked for help. She was a humble student, but had worked extremely hard and found success in her studies. She had a dream to become a nurse. She had finished high school several years earlier, but had been unable to figure out a way to pay for her post-secondary education. It is rare in Haiti to achieve a high school education, but even more shocking is the fact that 99% of Haitian high school grads do not go on to attend college. This is due exclusively to the financial hurdles.

> I told Nadege I was sorry that our country had failed her. I sincerely regretted that she could not use her strengths and skills to help her people. Unfortunately, I had to tell her that TeacHaiti was not able to give college scholarships. She was heartbroken, and so was I. Being the assertive woman that she is, she returned in 2008 with the same request. I proposed the idea to the TeacHaiti board of directors in Minnesota, and, as always, they supported the idea. TeacHaiti sent three college students to school in 2008, and two have already graduated with lab technology degrees. Both are currently working. Her graduation was an extremely proud day for me. In only three years, Nadege graduated from college with a Bachelor of Science in Nursing. She has been first in her class since her freshman year. She graduated summa cum laude on Sunday in a class of over 60 students. I was so proud to hear her exquisite valedictory speech. I tried hard to hold back the tears of joy. During her address, she heaped thanks upon

TeacHaiti. She is grateful that TeacHaiti believed in her competence and gave her a chance to make her nursing dreams come true.

Sponsors, thank you so much for making Nadege's dreams come true. We have added one competent nurse to the health care system in Haiti. I can say with confidence that Haiti is a better place because of her.

GLADYS SYLVESTRE THOMAS

In December of 2013, Miquette took us to the Hope Hospital in Port au Prince for an interview with a family and personal supporter of many years, Gladys Sylvestre Thomas. Miquette volunteers her services at the hospital one day a week to stay current in her nursing knowledge and skills. "Use it or lose it" Miquette says. While we were waiting for the interview, Miquette was scurrying about, helping, hugging, kissing and charming the staff. She is the quintessential people person.

The Hope Hospital is a private hospital where patients are required to pay for hospital services. It is bright, clean, in good repair, but in need of lab equipment. It was busy but not full. It was noted that a uniformed security person carrying a shotgun was patrolling the hallways and entrance to the hospital.

During the 2010 earthquake, the hospital was wide-open, free and packed, staffed by an emergency medical team flown in from the Quisqueya staging area by helicopters.

Given that Gladys Sylvestre has known the Denie family back since both families lived in St. Michel in the 1970's, one expected to meet an elderly matron. Instead, she is a brisk, energetic, full-speed-ahead, fast talking, upbeat and optimistic middle aged administrator.

Presently, she directs the Foundation for Children of Haiti which operates the Hospital of Hope, two orphanages and three schools. Children in the orphanages are in three groups: older children, children with severe disabilities (29 of them with physical and developmental needs) and a Rainbow of Love Nursery for young "abandoned for adoption" children, many of whom have been adopted by Minnesota families. Farah and Cherline Lee were in this orphanage along with Misha, the sister adopted by Canadians. Their older brothers, Pidens and Isaac were there too, temporarily, until Cleuis and Rose had enough food to feed them and could take them back.

The foundation is presently building a children's village where both orphanages and all the orphans will be. A new school is being built as well. The philosophy is that the schools are not free. Somebody has to pay. The intent is not to enable the children, but to empower them. They are hoping to educate the brightest kids to send them a long way toward building Haiti's future. When families get behind in tuition payments, the children are not sent home, but the families still owe.

Thomas was born and spent her early years in St. Michel, one of 10 children of a missionary father and mother, scrambling to feed their family. The family moved to Ohio and she spent her last year of high school there. Before she returned to Haiti nine years later, she became a nurse, got married, had two children and lived in Mississippi for a time.

When she returned in 1980, she volunteered at a needy orphanage operated by Christian Women in Action. She felt she had a God-given passion for kids and she and her husband adopted a four month old boy from the orphanage. Before long, the director of the orphanage left. The board offered her the job of running it. Her husband told her "You always wanted to do that." She felt she had heard the voice of God and took the job.

I'm Not Leaving Until You Give Me Food

The orphanage was operated out of a small rented house. Abandoned children (called "found" children) and dying children were being dropped off at the doorstep. The home filled quickly. A man named Richard Klein from California said "You need a bigger home" and donated $25,000 to buy one. Volunteers filled the home with used furniture. Then Thomas went out into the business places and the neighborhood begging for food, clothes, material and anything else useful. She was persistent: "I'm not leaving until you give me food."

The orphanage had its hands full. They found themselves running to the hospital with sick and damaged children. At one point, they had a measles epidemic in which seven children died because the hospital could not take them. Because of that, they undertook to build a children's hospital, scraping up $2000 to get the ball rolling.

Thomas operated during the regimes of Pappa Doc and Baby Doc Duvalier and Jean Bertrand Aristide. Their governments offered no financing, no help and no encouragement (but no discouragement)—total indifference to the plight of the orphans and the mission of the orphanage and hospital.

When Miquette's mother, Rose, moved to Port au Prince in 1989, she immediately got a job working in the Haiti Home for Children, working with handicapped children. This is how Thomas eventually came to know Pidens, Isaac, Farah, Cherlene, John and Mary Lee, and, eventually Miquette.

When John Lee met Miquette, he recognized her potential and asked Thomas "How can we help Miquette come to the United States to study?" Thomas tested Miquette, agreed with Lee's optimism and helped Miquette establish a connection with the Rotary Club in Port au Prince. Miquette was not of the class of student normally endorsed by the Rotary, but she proved herself.

Thomas says Miquette has founded an "educational ministry," and is doing all the right things to change the Haitian mindset—to put more value in education and to teach each family that without education there is almost no opportunity in Haiti for their children.

CHAPTER 15

MIQUETTE'S FAMILY

"I don't care how poor a man is, if he has a family, he's rich."

—Dan Wilcox and Thad Mumford

Let us return to Miquette's mother, Rose Denie. After Rose surrendered Farah and Cherline in 1989, she had another daughter, Camisha, born in 1991. Before the child was even born, arrangements had been made at the orphanage for her to go there. Rose delivered the baby alone at home at 8:00 a.m., cut her own umbilical cord, then delivered the child to the orphanage at 1:00 p.m. the same day. Camisha was adopted by a family in Canada and is now Camisha Jackson, living in Vancouver, British Columbia.

John Lee came to Haiti in 1999 to meet the Denie family. Miquette brought her mother to the guest house where John was staying where they both met him for the first time. Later Miquette and Rose took him to the Denie home to meet the rest of their family. Miquette was 18 going on 19 at that time. She had only completed school through the 10th grade.

The Denies and Miquette were all excited by John's proposal that Miquette come to the U.S. for a year of school. Arrangements were made, complicated arrangements, "jumping through hoops" and Miquette was allowed to go to the U.S. in 2000. She had been granted a one year student visa. Rose was pleased—she knew Miquette would be back in a year.

After a year Miquette was back, but this time with dreams of returning to the U.S. to finish high school and attend college. The Denie family had never dreamed of a child of theirs attending college so they were proud and excited at the prospect. But would they ever see her again? Rose was confident she would be back. Gladys Sylvestre Thomas had guaranteed U.S. customs she would have a job for Miquette when she returned and Miquette had promised to return.

Miquette kept in close contact with her family when she was attending high school and college in the U.S. She sent letters, cassettes and tapes, she scrimped on her expenses and sent part of her allowance home.

It had been a goal of Rose's that she would learn to read and write once her children were out of school. So in 2000 she hired a private tutor and took lessons for a year and a half. She was tutored for three hours three times a week for $12.50 each month. She also did some cooking and cleaning for her tutor. She was still working at the time. She was so proud and excited at the end of her studies to be able to endorse her own name on her paycheck.

After Miquette graduated from Concordia College, she spent a year in Detroit Lakes, working as a nurse at the hospital and nursing home. Rose knew she'd be back because Miquette had promised. But Rose understands that Farah, employed in a social services position in the Twin Cities and Cherline, now in the medical school at The University of Wisconsin, will not be expected to return to Haiti to live.

John and Mary Lee continue to be godsends for the Denie family. They sponsored Isaac through his graduation from medical school at the Joseph

Lafoture University in Port au Prince. Rose says Isaac would never have been able to go to medical school without the Lee sponsorship.

I Have a Chicken for You

Rose has visited the TeacHaiti School of Hope many times. After all, Dens and his wife, Chantal work there along with Beatrice. Many people come to Rose and ask for favors relating to the School of Hope. People tell her they are praying for her, Miquette and the school. Sometimes she gets compliments about the school while, Miquette, standing beside her, is ignored. "You have done so many good things. I have a chicken for you."

CLEUIS DENIE
A Better Carpenter than Jesus

Miquette's father, Cleuis Denie, died October 1st of 2013. Fortunately, we were able to interview him in March of 2013 when he was full of life and joy. The following account was written shortly after that interview.

If you want to spend an enjoyable hour in Haiti, arrange to talk to Cleuis Denie, Miquette's dad. But prepare to laugh and prepare for many family jokes in Creole that leave the interviewer out of the joke wondering what's so funny.

Cleuis was born in May 1, 1933, and since then has lost most of his hair and teeth, but not his sense of humor. He came from a poor family that had no money to send him to school. Their only income was from his mother selling coffee beans. When he was 8 years old, Cleuis went to live in the home of a judge in St. Michel. He did chores for the judge's family, but still no money

177

was available for school. He was learning carpentry. He left that home at age 17 and went to carpentry school, living with friends and acquaintances. He says he became a carpenter because Jesus was a carpenter. Then he jokingly says he's probably a better carpenter than Jesus was because he's had more experience. He's spent his entire working life making tables and chairs, doing tin roofs and anything carpentry-related, but no electrical or plumbing work. He says he's still strong and still working as a handy-man and that he's the jack of all trades (jack-a-tout mache in Creole).

When Cleuis was interviewed, Miquette acted as interpreter, but his wife Rose, son Dens, daughters Sandra and Beatrice were in the room along with other family members and Cleuis was clowning and having a great time. Jokes and laughs were flying in all directions, but no interpretations were offered, so only the interviewer was in the dark.

When Cleuis was a young man, he had a girlfriend, but he says "it didn't work out." So he prayed to God that he would meet somebody right away and he met Rose two weeks later. When they got serious about marriage, Rose told Cleuis he'd have to get permission from her parents. His own parents had died by then. Cleuis was terrified at the prospect and asked a more mature man to approach Rose's parents to vouch for him. The guy said "you'll have so pay me to do that." Cleuis refused but found another guy to do the job. The friend agreed, made the pitch, and after some delay and more dating, the deal was made and Cleuis and Rose were married. She was 16 years younger than he was. Talking to the two of them and gathering history from the rest of the family, it is clear that the pair are in dramatic contrast from one another. Cleuis is laid back, mischievous, easy going and funny, while Rose is more serious, a planner and an organizer, quite obviously the chief family decision maker. Miquette appears to have inherited the best qualities of each.

The first connection the Denie family had with America is when the little girls Farah and Cherline, were adopted by John and Mary Lee. Cleuis says that God chose the Lee family for his daughters and he's so happy they're doing so well. He says when he met the Lees and got to know them, "They showed me they are people who are following Christ."

When Miquette got the opportunity to go to the U.S. for school, Cleuis considered this a "gift from God," and it certainly has produced good results. If Miquette had stayed in America, she would have had a much better life, but he's so happy she chose to return to Haiti.

Cleuis and Miquette have a special relationship going back to the days when Rose and the other children had to leave St. Michel to go to Port au Prince to find work, leaving Cleuis and Miquette behind. When boys showed an interest in Miquette, she warned them "Don't mess with my dad, he has big guns (hands)." Indeed he has. It was hard for Rose to leave, but the family was relying on God to help her find a job and send back money when things were going slowly in the carpentry business. Cleuis was confident. He says "Life is not perfect, but if you have faith and do good, you will be happy." He's not a worrier. Cleuis says God gave him and Rose these wonderful children and he's so grateful and proud. He's sure they'll be world famous.

Cleuis has visited the TeacHaiti School of Hope many times and he's impressed and proud of the school, the program, and, of course, what Miquette had done and is doing.

Cleuis' health has taken several setbacks in recent years. He had a touch of cholera late in 2010 that knocked him off his feet temporarily. Then he had a slight stroke affecting his right side, but leaving no obvious symptoms. Then finally, pedestrian accidents. He has twice been hit by autos. But, he says he's "tough as a goat" and has prayed for the drivers who hit him.

PIDENS (DENS) DENIE

 Pidens "Dens" Denie is Miquette's brother, seven years older. He's a tall, good looking, well-built guy who loves to laugh, just like his dad. He's a full-time mechanic and driver at the Quesqueya Christian School and frequent designated-driver for TeacHaiti guests, visiting mission volunteers, and other school projects. He drives like a daring stunt pilot—fast, fearless, warnings ("look out puppy…thanks puppy"), honks, slipping in and out of traffic, darting through narrow openings, bluffing and practicing all the secrets and tricks of the Haitian driving culture. Riding with Dens—radio going and jokes flying—is a tense experience. Relaxation is impossible. But he never missed a shortcut, never missed a back street, never missed a bump and always got us safely to our destinations.

Dens is a key player in the Denie family that is a big factor in the TeacHaiti operation. He was born in St. Michel and went through the first four grades there. Then he moved to Port au Prince in 1993 to live with his mother Rose while he continued to go to school. When his dad, Cleuis, came down with Miquette from St. Michel to Port au Prince a few years later, Dens worked part-time with Cleuis as a carpenter, earning enough to pay for his own education. Father and son were building picnic tables, benches for schools, piggy bank boxes and collection boxes.

Tap Tap Driver

Dens went from 5th through 11th grade at Port au Prince, then left school. He wanted to go to trade school but didn't have the means. He became a tap tap (taxi) driver for three years. He rented the tap tap which is a covered pickup with a box and benches. Each bench holds seven people, 14

180

for a full cab, or sometimes more as some passengers sit on laps or stand on a platform at the end of the box and just hold on. Each tap tap has a designated route, point A to point B, and they don't deviate. Then it turns around and retraces the route. If a passenger wants to go somewhere off the route, he or she has to get off and take another tap tap. The fare is the equivalent of 10 -15 cents and cheating is rare. When passengers get off, they come around to the front and pay the driver. If the tap tap leaves too soon, some passengers are seen running to catch the tap tap to pay. A tap tap driver can probably earn enough to feed his family and that's about it. If you observe a fully loaded tap tap on a hot August day with passengers stuffed in, arm pit to arm pit, and some hanging off the back, no air conditioning, you can imagine you're watching a crowded sauna on wheels bumping down the street. The passengers who can move their arms are mopping their brows.

There are also motorcycle taxis that carry one, two or three passengers squeezed on the seat behind the driver. These taxis do not follow a particular route and can take passengers wherever they want to go.

Dens enrolled in a mechanic school while he was still driving tap taps. He went to class for afternoon sessions. In 2009 he switched to the morning session. When the earthquake struck in January of 2010, it came during an afternoon session. The big building where the school was housed, a trade school offering classes in mechanics, welding and carpentry, collapsed and all students in the afternoon classes, over 1000 of them, were killed.

After the earthquake, the Quisqueya School was closed from January through May of 2010 to provide a central staging location for emergency medical personnel coming in from outside the country. Most faculty staff members went to the United States. Many students went to the Dominican Republic. A few students stayed and took classes in school apartments.

Miquette was coordinating medical relief, directing doctors, nurses and health care professionals from all over the world to where they were most needed. Art was handling logistics. Interpreters were needed and some office people were on hand for detail work. Dens was hired as a driver along with five others during that period. They picked up medical volunteers at the airport, hauled them to the Quisqueya School for supplies and direction, then taxied them to hospitals and sites where their medical skills were needed. Some personnel and provisions were carried by the U.S. Marine helicopters flying in and out of the Quisqueya grounds.

After May, Quisqueya began to transition back to its normal programming. Dens, just a driver up to that time, was trained as a full time employee because of his mechanical background as well as his driving. Only one other driver was retained. Dens is the only mechanic. Quisqueya has five vehicles to maintain and Dens also maintains two TeacHaiti vehicles and drives for TeacHaiti, not as a full-time employee, but on an ad hoc basis. If you could ride across the streets and roads of Haiti for one day, you would understand why a full-time mechanic is needed to keep five vehicles running.

Dens is married, and he and his wife Chantal have four children. He is proud of the work he does for TeacHaiti because many children in Haiti never get the opportunity to go to school and he's happy to be part of a program that helps. He's also proud that Miquette is his sister. But, he says, "Proud doesn't say enough—there should be a bigger, better word." He says Miquette manages people so well. She holds them responsible and accountable so they don't need constant supervision. "They love her so much," he says.

Dens speaks Creole and knows just enough English, so that with a little help, he can be interviewed without an interpreter. Though it seems his best jokes, the ones that make him giggle the most, are in Creole. But, he hopes to travel to the United States with Miquette so he can learn more English.

CHANTAL DENIE

Chantal Denie is Dens' wife and the mother of their four children, one of whom, Guervens, age 6, is a first grader at the School of Hope.

Chantal is one of 12 siblings, but only two are left—the rest died in infancy or died young. Her education was through the 11th grade but she also went to a trade school for culinary training and has also taken a basic computer training program.

Chantal is employed by TeacHaiti. She is the school secretary and co-ordinator of scholarship programs. She organizes meetings and generally makes the program run. Miquette says the program would not run without Chantal. Miquette says if her plane plunged into the sea, Chantal could run the school without her. She has been employed by TeacHaiti since the beginning, 2007, three years before the School of Hope opened to the neighborhood kids. Payments to other schools for students sponsored by TeacHaiti are delivered personally by Chantal as part of her duties—because there is no mail service in Haiti. Chantal says the School of Hope gets many compliments and she takes personal pride for her role in the program.

Chantal is paying for Guervens' education and is so impressed that strangers are willing to pay for the education of Haitian children.

Chantal says Miquette doesn't have to pray for herself because so many others are already praying for her.

SANDRA DENIE

Sandra Denie is an older sister of Miquette. She lives in Port au Prince. Miquette says Sandra was vital in sending her to America. She not only encouraged it, but she, along with her sister, Beatrice and brother Dens all chipped in to pay for a private tutor for Miquette who needed tutoring to learn English so she could go to America. The tutoring was daily.

Sandra is a strong supporter of education for the children of Haiti. Her mother, Rose, pushed her hard to go to school and she enjoyed it. She has graduated from high school and has had one year of college studying finance. She calls herself a merchant. She has a business she conducts from her home, selling food products, cooking supplies spices and cleaning products. She says she would be unable to conduct her business if she had not been educated. She says her education multiplied her potential and that without it she would be unoccupied and "useless." Her husband, Lusnord, went to school through the 7th grade, then later went to a tailor training program for 1 ½ years and is now occupied as a tailor.

Sandra and her husband have two sons and four daughters. She forced her 22 year old son, John Benson, to go to school, which he quit after the 11th grade. Later he went to one year of plumbing school and now has a job as a plumber. He loves it. Sandra's four daughters are 6, 9, 16 and 20 years old. All are in school and her family pays tuition to keep them there. She says her 16 year old daughter, Santia, would be a street kid or maybe washing clothes day to day if she weren't in school.

The subject of restaveks comes up often in interviews in Haiti. The family next door to Sandra and her family has a 10 year old girl at their house, a restavek. The girl gets up before anybody else in the morning to fetch water, and she eats last—the leftovers. She takes the family's older child to school. The restavek might be a cousin or a niece. These restaveks are mostly girls from the countryside and have a miserable existence. When restaveks are relatives, they sometimes get better treatment, but there are no guarantees.

President Michel ("Sweet Micky") Martelly has been president only since May of 2011, but he has done many good things so far according to Sandra. He is building roads, making businesses pay taxes, encouraging education and he has even started some public schools. He is trying to decentralize Haiti and has moved an annual festival from Port au Prince, where it had been held every year, to Cap Haitian, on the coast, and to a different major city every year, to spread the benefits.

Sandra was living in Port au Prince during the earthquake and was terrified when she felt the shock wave, but was unhurt. She has since moved her family and business about an hour away where the business could operate better.

When the cholera epidemic followed later that year, 2010, her father, Cleuis, then 77 years old, contracted the disease, had near-seizures and was taken to the hospital where he recovered. Because of the national emergency, there was no charge for the doctors and the hospital. Cleuis had a stroke in early 2013 and was taken to the hospital again where he was treated on an outpatient basis and released. The family was charged for the hospital tests.

When John and Mary Lee adopted Farah and Cherline, the family knew it was a necessary step, but they were sad. Dens came home and they were gone. He hadn't been told it would happen. He cried because he loved his sisters. Their brother, Isaac, had the same experience.

Sandra is "very proud" of Miquette and what she is doing at the School of Hope. She gets very animated just talking about it. She says Miquette didn't have to come back to Haiti, but she did and now she's helping so many, including her family. Sandra says Miquette "is a mother with many children."

Miquette says Sandra was always helping her family and when Miquette was in school, Sandra was always on hand to provide money when it was short. Now, Sandra says, the family comes to Miquette for help.

Miquette was a translator for Sandra's interview, at their parents' home, but now Sandra is going to school again, taking classes in English.

BEATRICE DENIE

Beatrice Denie is the biological mother of Cherline Denie (now Lee), but was 16 when Cherline was born and Cherline quickly became Rose's daughter. But, Rose was sick at the time and had no job and no money. Rose and Beatrice agreed that the situation was impossible and they'd have to agree to an adoption.

Beatrice has been employed by the School of Hope since the school opened in September of 2010. She works full time as kitchen supervisor which includes cooking. Before that she worked as a street merchant selling sandals, shoes, underwear, and food products such as rice, beans, and oil. Street vending is not a satisfactory occupation and is discouraged by the mayor of Port au Prince in an effort to improve the image of the city. Sometimes the inventory is confiscated by the city and totally lost. Vendors are encouraged to sell, if they must, out of their own homes, but there is no profit in home sales. This uncertainty was stressful and Beatrice is happy to be out of the street merchant business and getting a regular paycheck.

The way street vending works is for the vendors to go to a warehouse early in the morning where wholesalers sell the vendors the merchandise that will be sold on the streets. The margins are narrow. The vendors either walk to and from the warehouses, or if the distance is too great, they must take tap-taps to and from the warehouse, further reducing the profit margin. This interviewer met a warehouse owner from Gonaives in the Miami airport. He was just returning from Trenton, New Jersey, were he said he bought a large supply of what he called "cheap, used" merchandise to bring back to Haiti to sell to street merchants. This middle man gave the impression that he's the one making real money from street merchandising.

Because of family finances and frequent sickness, Beatrice only got through the 7th grade in school which limited her opportunities. Now she is seeing the opportunities being provided by the School of Hope and is proud to be part of the program. She says the school is "a huge favor God has done for us—we give credit to God."

She says it is humbling when parents say they can't believe their children get to go to school at TeacHaiti to learn to read and write, get to eat, and learn to use silverware. She says the name TeacHaiti is respected. Parents talk to other parents about how good the school is, so now, Beatrice says, the richer parents want to send their children to this school where the poor children are going. Beatrice heard one mother telling her little daughter, pointing to Miquette, "She went to school, now you can see what she's able to do." As a result, Beatrice says, she brags about Miquette.

Cherline was the first grandchild in the family and they all loved her. Miquette babysat the little girl. Now Beatrice has been returning the favor since Miquette's son Maxwell was born and she looks forward to the day when she can hold Cherline's babies.

On the day of the earthquake, January 10, 2010, Beatrice had several places she planned to go to get a birth certificate she needed because her old one was damaged and she needed a new one. This task would have taken her to several downtown buildings. But she became uneasy and a voice told her "You need to stay away." So she postponed. That afternoon, two buildings she had planned to visit were totally destroyed with people dying in the wreckage.

Beatrice's daughter, Nadege, was 20 at the time of the earthquake. When the quake hit, Nadege jumped to safety from the first floor of her school. The building collapsed behind her. She saw a classmate die in front of her. Nadege and Cherline are half sisters.

Cherline is now in medical school at the University of Wisconsin and Beatrice is so happy for her and proud of her. Cherline has visited the Denie family in Haiti twice. Beatrice says this is a family that loves one another and helps one another.

DR. ISAAC DENIE

Miquette's brother, Isaac Denie, 29 years old in December, 2013, is the seventh in line of the nine children of Cleuis and Rose Denie. He left St. Michel at the age of six to live with his mother in Port au Prince. Cleuis and Miquette followed when they were able.

From the time he was just a child it was Isaac's dream to become a doctor. He was always fascinated by his studies in biology and ecology. But, for financial reasons, he didn't graduate from high school until he was 23. Some of his help came from Miquette, scrimping on her allowance in the U.S., then later from her wages at the

Emmanuel Nursing Home and St. Mary's Hospital. After his high school graduation, Isaac took computer training at the ENUP Technical School in Port au Prince. His expenses there were paid by John and Mary Lee.

He entered medical school where he spent three years at the Haitian Academy University. Then he transferred for a final year at the Joseph Laforture University, graduating with an M.D. in September, 2013, though he is still required to do a two year residency in a countryside location which he started in January of 2014. His medical school expenses were provided by John and Mary Lee. The residency will be sponsored by the Haitian government which will provide a modest stipend (enough for cheese sandwiches, said Isaac, but no meat). Again, he will receive supplemental income from John and Mary Lee.

Dr. Denie's goal is to pursue a specialty in neurosurgery. He says presently there are no neurosurgeons in Haiti. All neurosurgeons have left Haiti for greener pastures. He acknowledged that there are more Haitian surgeons in Montreal, Canada than in all of Haiti. He ultimately plans to go to Cuba (now providing the best medical care in the Caribbean) for neurosurgical training.

Dr. Denie feels well prepared to deliver high level medical care because he received high level medical training from American and Cuban doctors. He says the medical education in Haiti is the same as in America and Cuba. But see the information provided in the Health in Haiti Chapter 18 of this book.

Denie is familiar with the new, state-of-the-art hospital operated by Dr. Paul Farmer's Partners in Health in Mirbalais, Haiti. He aspires to actually practice there in the future, though his acquaintances in St. Michel wish for him to return there to practice.

Health care is more accessible in the Dominican Republic than it is in Haiti, which is one reason Denie is determined to stay in Haiti, following the example of his sister, Miquette who brought her training and talents home. He now lives in Port au Prince with his wife, Ruth, and their six year old son.

With regard to Miquette's work, Isaac has visited the School of Hope often and has been impressed by the obvious talent and intelligence of the children there. He feels TeacHaiti is doing an amazing job helping the families and children of that poor neighborhood. He says the more children who are educated in Haiti, the stronger Haiti will be.

Two Haitian physical characteristics were discussed with Dr. Denie. The first was the conspicuously (to an American) rare appearance of obesity among Haitian children and adults. Isaac indicated that it is a medical fact that when people sweat during hot days, their metabolism is higher—burning more calories. He also pointed out that because of the poverty of the general population, there is less money for rich foods and snacks. He did not speculate as to whether there is a genetic factor, a Haitian body type. But the streets and sidewalks are covered with folks who have slender trunks and limbs. Women are thin, but shapely and men are generally lean.

Another observation was that despite poor diet, the Haitian people appear to have amazingly excellent teeth—straight (as though they had been straightened by orthodontists—which they haven't), and pearly white with no teeth missing. In his own case, Dr. Denie says he has always taken good care of his teeth, even when food was short. But in addition to that, he says that the drinking water in Haiti is rich with tropical minerals that foster strong and healthy teeth.

Isaac Denie presents a strong contrast with his brother, Pidens, in several ways. Physically, older brother, Dens is tall and muscular, about 6'2" and

190

200 pounds. Isaac is shorter and quite slim, maybe 5'10" and under 130 pounds. There is an even greater contrast in their personalities. Pidens is outgoing, laughing, joking and joyously noisy—just like his late father, Cleuis. Isaac is sober, quiet, serious, and composed—more like his mother, Rose, though Rose is probably not as reserved as her seventh child.

MIQUETTE'S AMERICAN SISTERS

FARAH LEE

Farah (pronounced Far-ah, not Fair-ah) Lee is a younger sister of Miquette, brought to the United States at the age of four in 1989 and adopted by John and Mary Lee.

When Miquette first arrived in Detroit Lakes, Farah was 15 and just entering high school—the 9th grade. She had so many anxieties about Miquette coming. She remembers the night of arrival very well. She and Cherline were upstairs in the Lee house, nervous and reluctant to come down. Her first impression of Miquette were that she was so skinny and was wearing a beautiful dress. She had only one bag. Farah just stared at her—"this is my sister."

Miquette Wasn't Cool

Farah's anxiety about starting high school was only heightened by this 20 year old sister who would only be a junior. What will this be like? How will I answer the puzzling questions by the other kids? Miquette seemed to know very little English and she didn't have many clothes—she wasn't cool. Farah didn't want to be the person responsible for explaining what Miquette was all about. She was not crazy about the whole idea but she felt cornered. Then there was the incident where Miquette held up a Tampax and wondered what that was all about. That didn't help Farah's embarrassment.

Farah was successful in track the next spring—running the 100m, 200m, relay and long jumping. Her Lakers qualified for the State Track Team meet which was a blast. Miquette was athletic too and wanted to run track, but at age 20, she was not eligible because she was too old.

Miquette's arrival wasn't easy for Cherline either, either in school or in the community. The sisters struggled to teach Miquette how to use the internet. Looking back, Farah admits she isn't proud of the way she handled her older sister's arrival. The sisters grew closer as Miquette explained that the difficulties of their Haitian family forced the family to allow Farah and Cherline to be adopted and how hard it was on their parents to let them go.

Then when the Lee family set off to Haiti a year later to renew Miquette's visa, the three sisters, Farah, Cherline and Miquette were pulled together and became close friends as well. So when Miquette went to Oak Grove the next year, Farah and Cherline were disappointed they would be separated from their sister, their new best friend.

She has seen her biological mother, Rose, three times since leaving Haiti as a four year old. The first time was in 2001, at the age of 15 when the entire Lee family went to Haiti so that Miquette, after one year in the U.S., could renew her visa. When the Lees arrived at the airport in Port au Prince, the situation was most awkward. It was very hot, there was no place to sit and John Lee and Miquette, being driven by their brother, Dens, had to leave almost immediately to line up an appointment. That left Farah, Cherline, Mary, Daniel and Carl Lee with Rose. The Lees couldn't speak Creole and Rose couldn't speak English. There were no interpreters. Farah was overwhelmed—filled with emotion, feeling she had so much to say but no way of saying it. Farah felt people in the airport were staring at them—two African-American children (she doesn't think of herself as Haitian-American) with white parents.

It was awkward for Farah visiting Haiti at age 15 for other reasons. She felt anxiety about how close to get to her biological family because her adoptive parents were always present. She was so happy to be there, but reluctant to express her feelings. She was holding back—felt she was in a weird place as an adopted child. Should she call Rose "Mother" or Rose? Should she call Cleuis "Dad" or Cleuis? She was uncomfortable in conversations, unhappy—everybody was listening. Miquette was busy translating, but wanted to reconnect as well. Farah hadn't been all that close to Miquette on that first year Miquette was in Detroit Lakes, but became very close on that trip to Haiti and feels they have been inseparable ever since.

When John Lee and Miquette returned to the airport with Dens, they were taken to a Guest House where the family would be staying. They had several dinners at Rose's house. The house was tiny but very clean. Rose was very gracious and provided huge meals. It was evident that Rose was very proud of her girls—Miquette, Farah and Cherline. The Lees also had several dinners at the home of older sister, Sandra, who has always lived in Haiti.

By the way, though Cherline was technically Farah's niece, she considers her a sister. Farah and Cherline were inseparable, growing up together in Haiti and have always been sisters.

When Farah was a little girl in Haiti, she was sickly. She had many seizures. The family couldn't afford standard medical care with doctors and hospitals, so Rose engaged herbalists for home treatment. She didn't know what to do. Farah had one such seizure in Detroit Lakes at the age of four. Her eyes rolled back and she was rushed to Fargo for emergency treatment. There has never been a diagnosis that Farah knows about, no seizures, no treatment since that incident and no medications.

Farah says Rose knew in her heart she was doing the right thing by putting the girls up for adoption—there was nothing else she could do. She feels it was God's plan for the family and she has no regrets. It probably helps that the girls have been raised by a wonderful family, a solid family and would be educated and probably get good jobs. She learned more about the background of why she was adopted back in 2009. It was the story of a small house, limited food, poverty, sickness and desperation—no choice.

The girls' dad, Cleuis, was as thrilled to see his daughters as they were to see him. Cleuis was 16 years older than Rose, in his 70's, and still working as a carpenter. When he saw them, Cleuis said, "Now that I have finally seen my girls. I can die in peace." But Cleuis was very much against the adoption originally. Remember, he didn't sign any consent papers. Cleuis and Rose were not on speaking terms for weeks after his two little girls were sent to the U.S.. Cleuis showed pure joy with the girls. Farah says it was clear that he had great pride in what they were doing. He knew in his heart too that the adoption was the right thing.

Farah's impression of Port au Prince at the age of 15 was not a culture shock. She knew it would be destitute and it was. She was struck by the amount of trash on the streets and in the ditches. The traffic was chaotic. But she loved the spirit. The people were so poor, but they were genuinely happy and resilient. She thinks their faith in God carries them through their poverty. She noted that she didn't see many elderly people on the streets because Haiti has such a low life expectancy.

After graduation from high school in Detroit Lakes, Farah attended South-west University of Minnesota at Marshall, MN, graduating in 2009 with a bachelor's degree in social work. Her first job was with Tasks Unlimited in Minneapolis as a mental health coordinator doing one-on-one work direct-ly with clients on coping with mental illness. She found the work exciting and challenging.

Farah's second return trip to Haiti was 10 years later, in March 2011. At that time, all her original brothers and sisters were out of school. Older brother Dens had learned a good deal of English. Her nephew, Cleeford, about 12 years old, was living with Rose and Cleuis. Her nephew, John Benson, a son of older sister, Sandra, was also close to the family. At age 25, Farah re-turned alone for six days. Miquette had kept inviting her and now that she was finished with college, had a stable job, and could afford to go, she went. The job: Farah is employed in Hennepin County by People Incorporated as a case manager and vocational specialist providing mental health treatment for homeless people and the mentally ill.

This trip was entirely different. She felt at home this time. Her brother, Dens, picked her up at the airport and joked with her. She had a very good feeling. Though she was apprehensive because of the 2010 earthquake, her fear of the unknown was gone. No longer a 15 year old teenager, but a mature young lady without anxiety. It was so much easier to talk to Rose and Cleuis with her adoptive parents not present, though she still needed Miquette to interpret. Rose and Cleuis asked about Farah's job—which was good—and they were still very proud. She was successful in their eyes.

A feature of this second trip was that members of the original family, Dens, Rose, Isaac, John Benson (age 20), a TeacHaiti teacher, and Farah took a trip back to the original family home in St. Michel, five hours north. They all rode in a pickup driven by Dens. St. Michel is about the size of Frazee,

Minnesota says Farah and is in the mountains. The actual size of St. Michel is a puzzle.

It was a fun trip with the road going through some very primitive villages. At one point they found themselves in need of water. Miquette recruited some local children to help her get a gallon. Miquette rewarded the children with lollipops from a supply she had brought along. One mother told her those lollipops may be the only food those kids would get that day.

They revisited the original family house where Farah had lived the first three years of her life. Miquette and Art have remodeled the house and stay there when they travel to St. Michel. They met some of the old friends, neighbors who remembered Farah and Cherline as toddlers. They saw some children splashing in a puddle. Miquette told Farah that she and Cherline used to play in puddles just like that. They also met Miquette's elementary school teacher and met Rose's brother, Tayan, and his wife. Tayan was the uncle who had made good—a family with new clothes and plenty of food.

Farah felt the two day trip to St. Michel was a time for her to connect the dots of her early days in Haiti. When she left to return to the U.S., Rose held onto her like she didn't want her to go (just as she had over 20 years earlier). The emotions of this farewell were heartbreaking for Farah.

Farah's third return trip to Haiti was only eight months later, November 2011. This was a four day fun trip for Miquette's wedding. Big sister was marrying Art McMahon, a school teacher from Ohio, on the same faculty as Miquette at the Quesqueya Christian School in Port au Prince. It was a memorable occasion. All the Lees from Detroit Lakes, Art's family from Ohio and the original Denie family were all there. The families were talking and laughing, having a great time together and exclaiming what blessings they all were for one another.

Farah and Cherline were bridesmaids for Miquette along with one of Miquette's Haitian friends. The bridesmaids had their hair fixed professionally at a salon and the families stayed at first class, immaculate hotels. The sisters and friends even spent a day at the beach with Art and Miquette. While she was there, Farah visited the TeacHaiti School, saw the happy kids, saw the raising of the flag, saw the results of the work and felt she has seen a miracle. It was a short trip, but a great family event for Farah.

Farah now calls Miquette "a blessing in my life." Reconnecting with her childhood in Haiti cemented the relationship. If Miquette were not in Haiti, Farah would probably not return again. She says Miquette is a great and cherished "go-to" person for personal questions and discussions because she is so wise and patient. She has the "soul of a 90 year old." She says that if she had to describe Miquette in one word, that word would be "grace."

Farah added that John and Mary Lee are an amazing couple—big hearted, friendly, patient—she can't imagine any other parents.

CHERLINE LEE

Miquette's sister, Cherline Lee is 28 years old now and a first year student at the University of Wisconsin Medical School. She went to college at the mostly black Tuskagee University in Tuskagee, Alabama and graduated in 2009 with a degree in biology, then did research for three years at the Mayo Clinic in Rochester, Minnesota. Her current program at the University of Wisconsin is an MBPT program in which she will end up with an MD degree and PhD in research in the biological sciences.

Cherline has been back to Haiti three times: the Lee family trip in 2001 when she was 15 years old in August, 2010, after the earthquake, and briefly in 2011 for Miquette and Art's wedding.

In 2010, she spent about a month in Haiti helping teachers organize the opening of the new School of Hope. She went to "give back." She said she felt guilty to be living a life of privilege in the United States when great suffering was taking place in Haiti. She had felt the need to give back ever since visiting Haiti as an 8th grader in 2001. Mostly, she was assisting English teacher, Bilybert Audige, in preparation for his teaching duties. She was very impressed with Bily.

Her impressions of Haiti, just seven months after the quake, were dramatic. She saw rubble where homes had been. She saw open spaces where buildings had been. The capitol building was destroyed. She could remember when this symbol of unity had been standing. It hit her hard to see it crumbled. She reacted emotionally to the tent cities, especially around the airport and capitol building. She felt all this devastation had occurred just when Haiti was getting better. "What a slap in the face." But the Haitians were so happy. They had adjusted. She saw many with arms or legs missing, but they seemed to be getting along so well. And the children in school who had gone through so much were happy and optimistic.

As Cherline visited her Haitian family, relatives and old neighbors, they struggled through the language barriers as Cherline spoke only English now and the Haitians spoke Creole. As she became reacquainted with Beatrice, her biological mother, and Beatrice's daughter, Nadege, Cherline's half-sister, she could see their personalities and hers were closely related: quiet, even-keel, laid-back, introspective and not necessarily laughing out loud at every joke.

Cherline's impressions of the newly opened School of Hope were that it was small and cramped, but it had an actual, functioning flushing toilet and shower. The children had to be taught how to use the toilet. The kids were so happy and excited—smiling every day. They were all from the surrounding neighborhood, but they were hand-picked because they were smart and motivated. They dressed in their best shoes and pants. Their hair was neat and the girls had bows in theirs. These children lived in shantys, but were considered middle class. The kids on the streets who were not in school were just the opposite: in dirty tatters and rags. Without scholarships, they will remain the poorest of the poor. They can't even afford shoes and socks. Many of them will end up restaveks—servants or slaves.

You'd Be Eating Dirt.

Cherline reflected on what would have happened to her if she had never had the opportunities that flowed from her adoption by the Lees. She might not even be alive. There had been a huge struggle to feed children when she was surrendered to the orphanage. As Miquette joked "You'd be eating dirt." Instead, in 2012, she was deciding between medical research and medical practice.

Calculating, But Not Devious.

When Cherline was in Haiti, Miquette and Art treated her very well, including dinner at some very nice restaurants. Cherline claims it was so that she'd want to return to Haiti when her education is completed. She says Miquette is calculating but not devious. Cherline says she would love to return to Haiti to practice medicine among the Haitians, but there are many uncertainties in her life at this point that her future path is unclear.

Cherline said it is clear to her that Miquette is extremely driven. People in Haiti at the School of Hope and Quisqueya Christian School told her they were greatly impressed with what Miquette did immediately following the earthquake—coordinating medical services and providing medical care herself. She said that she could see that Miquette commands respect and that people are drawn to her. When Miquette arrived at the Lee home in 2000 she was a stranger to Cherline. They didn't even speak the same language. But by 2010, they were full sisters and Cherline was so proud of her.

Cherline observed differences between the students of the Quisqueya Christian School and the TeacHaiti School of Hope. She said the Quesqueya students appeared to be from wealthy families, judging by their clothes, the fact that many of them drove SUVs and very nice cars.

They struck her as privileged, some spoiled, and they looked just like American teenagers from the right side of the tracks who spoke English well, carried on conversations about a culture that wasn't Haitian and listened to American music. They aspired to go to college in France or America. These kids were often seen in fine restaurants. Watching them, Cherline felt she was in a twilight zone somewhere outside of Haiti.

Cherline was invited by Art to go along with the class on a senior trip up into the mountain area of Northern Haiti. The dwellings along the narrow mountain road were shanties—shacks. They passed a shed loaded with caskets. This was a funeral home. One building was a dirty little school about the size of a garage where kids of all ages were cramped inside singing an alphabet song. She said the Quisqueya students took no notice of the conditions because they don't understand the needs of the poor. They're living in Haiti, but "they're living in a bubble."

The children in the School of Hope, by contrast, were total strangers to the Quisqueya culture inside the bubble. Theirs was the day-to-day, hand-to-mouth existence.

Cherline became emotional on the subject of educating Haitian children. Without being prideful, she said "Look what happens when you give a Haitian kid the opportunity to be educated: look what Miquette is doing, look what Farah is doing and look at what I'm doing. Deny that education and you are sentencing a form of what—slavery, servanthood, selling in the streets, poverty, injury, death and a short life."

Cherline's observations and sensitivity suggest that, if circumstances allow, she might very well take her medical training back to Haiti to work for the Haitian people as her sister Miquette has done.

CHAPTER 16

SUPPORTERS IN ST. MICHEL

"It takes a village to raise a child."
—African Proverb

There are 80 TeacHaiti children in 10 or 15 schools in St. Michel. One is the TeacHaiti school where classes are held in a tent. Children are seen outside the tent, looking in, wishing they could go to school too. The other schools do not teach English until the 8th grade. The TeacHaiti School teaches English from the first grade on. In the TeacHaiti School and other schools where children attend with TeacHaiti scholarships, meals are included.

The educational system out in the rural areas of Haiti is even worse than in the cities. Teachers are poorly paid and paychecks are delayed because Haiti has no postal system.

But land is cheap in the countryside and Miquette owns a lot in St. Michel suitable for the construction of a permanent school building. Miquette, looking forward, is determined to build one, and eventually a trade school to generate local jobs on vacant property on the edge of town. Miquette is further determined that the best teachers, Haitians, will be hired to teach there and will be well paid.

The Fairfax Project

The St. Michel building project was on TeacHaiti's back burner until folks from the Fairfax Community Church (FCC) in Fairfield, Virginia traveled to Haiti to provide earthquake relief, met Miquette, saw what TeacHaiti had done in Port au Prince and heard Miquette's dream for a school in St. Michel.

The FCC is an evangelical congregation affiliated with the Church of God, Anderson, Indiana. The church has six full-time pastors, including a Pastor of Global Engagement. Their average weekly attendance is 2,158 worshipers. The City of Fairfax is a community of 22,000 located in the Washington, D.C. metropolitan area.

The Fairfax people have made many mission trips to Haiti. Somewhere in this process they connected with Miquette and visited the TeacHaiti School of Hope in Port au Prince and were impressed with the school, the program and the larger vision. The group provided the means and the labor in installing the playground and equipment of the second of the two School of Hope buildings.

In April of 2013, Fairfax sent a team to St. Michel to scope the area with the idea of building a TeacHaiti school in that village. The Fairfax team is headed by a dynamic engineer named Bill Zink who is directing the campaign with great zeal and energy. The team has produced a proposed floor plan for a school with six classrooms, space for 150 children, a cafeteria, kitchen, breezeways, playground and courtyard. During the 2013 Thanksgiving holiday, another team went to St. Michel to work on estimates and logistics for the actual construction. They are now back in Fairfax raising money for materials and are planning to send engineers and volunteer labor for the actual construction of the school. Hallelujah.

The Fairfax group is working in cooperation with the TeacHaiti board in Detroit Lakes. TeacHaiti board president, Tom Klyve and board member, Rhys Anderson and his wife, Sheila, traveled to Fairfax in October, 2013 to become acquainted, worship together and to discuss the vision and details. Most recently, Mr. Chris Dias, the full-time IT director of the FCC has been elected to the TeacHaiti board of directors and meets with them regularly by skype.

The urgent need and deep longing for more affordable classrooms for the poor children of St. Michel is heard in the voices of the parents and supporters in St. Michel who spoke to us in March of 2013.

ESTAYAN "TAYAN" ESTERILE

When Miquette was just growing up in St. Michel, Uncle Estayan "Tayan" Esterile, her mother's brother, was considered by Miquette to be the richest man in St. Michel. That's because Tayan, a carpenter who had a good business making and selling coffins, was a good provider for his own family and a generous uncle for his nieces and nephews.

Uncle Tayan's three children were well dressed, well fed and had a bike for going to school. Tayan would drop by Miquette's home (her mother was in Port au Prince and her father had already gone to work) and drop off a few coins to make sure Miquette, then 12-13 years old, would have some food for breakfast that day. Then Miquette would run to the market and pick something up. He also kept an eye on Miquette to make sure she didn't get into trouble. In reality, Tayan was not wealthy, but warm-hearted and caring.

He also saw to it that there was enough money to send his own children to school. The need for schools and education may be even more desperate in St. Michel than it is in Port au Prince. You might say St. Michel is "in the boonies" in Haiti. It is far off the beaten path, and believe it, the path to St. Michel is indeed beaten. In St. Michel there is little industry and few jobs, so seven out of eight children would be unable to go to school without help. Even with the help that is made available through TeacHaiti, half the children who should be in school are not. Tayan says those children either must find work on small family subsistence farms in the area or become thieves.

Within 12 months of our interview with Uncle Tayan, he had died. For Tayan, who once made three or four coffins in a day, business had slowed to a trickle because in the early years there were no funeral homes and business came directly to him. Now there are funeral homes which are not buying much of his product—maybe one a month. But, he was still is a strong supporter of schools, education and scholarships in St. Michel because he knew what happens to the children who shape their futures on the streets.

Some, mostly girls, become restaveks. Even poor people in the country have restaveks working on farms. They get shabby treatment, get up early, work harder than family and go to bed late. Why? They couldn't go to school, but when young women get educated, they get jobs and even birth rates go down.

PIERRE NOVRRY

TeacHaiti has a "go to" man in St. Michel who carries messages and money back and forth between St. Michel and Port au Prince and handles suggestions from parents and teachers. He's Pierre Novrry who has two children in the TeacHaiti School, Aima Anaelle, 6, (sponsored by this author and his wife) and Dave Abimael, age 7.

Novrry was Miquette's 2nd grade teacher, but having only an 11th grade education himself, he was earning so little, he became a tap-tap operator between St. Michel and Cape Haitian 42 miles away. He carries a load of up to 18 passengers.

Miquette says Pierre is "in charge." He meets with students and parents to see to it that the children are keeping up with their school work. He conducts parent meetings which the parents must attend. If the children don't maintain their grades, they can't return to school the following year. He carries messages from Miquette to the parents. He carries payroll and scholarship cash from Port au Prince to St. Michel and tuition fees back.

Pierre says that without sponsor tuition support, perhaps some children could afford to attend some of the cheaper private schools in St. Michelle, but not the good school that TeacHaiti is. His children enjoy the school very much. His daughter Aima started the year as a first grader but has progressed so much she has been advanced to the second grade. Her favorite activity is to read—in both French and Creole. His dreams for his children are that they become better educated than their father and that they will be able to go to the best schools and get the best education possible.

Pierre said that he prays for the sponsors of his children, giving thanks and praying that they will continue their support.

JUSTIN PIERRE

 Justin Pierre was a 6th grade teacher in St. Michel when Miquette was growing up. He was a neighbor of the Denie family. Although he has only a high school education, he has been a teacher ever since graduation—13 years. He didn't teach at Miquette's school, but he was a tutor on the side for extra income and tutored Miquette for an hour a day, five days a week, because her father, Cleuis, couldn't read or write and was unable to help her.

Mr. Pierre says "way too many" children in rural Haiti do not go to school because of finances. St. Michel does have a public school, but many cannot afford even to attend the public school because the school requires student uniforms and shoes.

Those who don't go to school just hang around the streets or get minimal jobs. Some steal and some end up in jails. Many of the girls become restaveks, run errands, fetch water, go to market, get pregnant between the ages of 12 and 15 and face a downhill future. Many boys get involved in rape situations although most assaults are not reported.

Of those fortunate enough to finish high school, most become teachers. Some dream of going to the college, but lack the means. He says the local Digicel office has hired some high school graduates at $90 per month which is considered a good salary. Local private schools pay teachers $50-$75 per month depending on experience.

Mr. Pierre is a strong supporter of the TeacHaiti program in St. Michel. He says Miquette was an excellent student when he tutored her (he is only 8 years older than his former student) and he is proud of what she is doing in her home town. "My work," he says "is being paid off."

ROLAND AND CELINE "VIDA" ALIX

  Roland and Celine, called "Vida," have two children in the TeacHaiti program in St. Michel, a girl, 10 and a boy, 13. Roland, who has gone to school through the 3rd grade, is an independent carpenter, making coffins, tables, bed frames and doing remodeling. Vida, who finished six grades, has no job but wishes she did.

They say their children love to read, but have no books and there is no library at their school. They want their children to become knowledgeable to learn a trade, to go to a university and to have a better life than their parents. They are thankful for the TeacHaiti program in St. Michel and are looking forward to the construction of an actual school.

EDITTE ALIX

Editte Alix lives in St. Michel. She was only able to complete six grades in school. She has no job. She supports the TeacHaiti program because it's helping the community. She says without an education it's hard to become anything because there is no way to open doors. Editte was helping in the home of Miquette in St. Michel when the other interviews were being conducted and said she wanted to be interviewed too. She is a sister of Roland Alix.

JOSEPH "TJOE" VAL

Since she was a little girl in St. Michel, Miquette has known Joseph "Tjoe" Val who had a small farm on the edge of town next to the Denie home. His chickens wandered over to the Denie yard and laid some of their eggs. Miquette would gather and protect the eggs. Then Tjoe would come looking—"Where are my eggs?" The eggs were returned to their owner, often with some food from the Denie stove, and sometimes Tjoe would come over to share food from his stove. Tjoe and his wife had seven children. Two were surrendered and adopted out with consent signatures by X and thumbprint the same as Miquette's sisters Farah and Cherline in 1998 and 1999.

Tjon's wife has died. Now he's 66 and poor. He never went to school at all and manages to eke out a living on his farm raising corn, yams, sweet potatoes, green beans and sorghum. He says he gets four crops a year. He was cheerful on the day of the interview because there was a good rain earlier that day.

Among his children, Tjon has two sons, 18 and 22 years old. Miquette encouraged him to put those sons in school so they could learn to read and write and break the cycle of poverty. They are both sponsored by TeacHaiti and both are in the 7th grade. Tjon wants them to learn enough to get into a trade school and get better jobs than farming.

Tjoe considered his interview important enough to wear a suit. He says there is no way his sons could be in school without scholarships from TeacHaiti. His gratitude, pride and respect are immense: "My sons are lucky to be getting something I never had."

Tjoe has great affection for Miquette. He remembers when she was a little girl running around the neighborhood naked. He appreciates that she still cares about the people in her old neighborhood and is working to make all of St. Michel go forward. He's proud of her loyalty.

NERLINE BRUTUS

Nerline Brutus and Miquette were neighbors in St. Michel, growing up together until Miquette left to go to Port au Prince at the age of 15. Her story here is included to demonstrate a common path a young woman's life can take in Haiti.

Nerline and Miquette didn't go to the same school. Nerline was unable to continue after she finished the 6th grade.

Nerline now has four living children from 2 to 18 years old. But Nerline's story is the story of the child who died. In 1996, Nerline was pregnant and living with an abusive boyfriend—abusive even when she was pregnant. The plan was that when the baby (boy as it turned out) came, he would be taken to an orphanage in Port au Prince and surrendered. But, Nerline kept the baby until he was six months old. At that point they were starving and the baby had to be taken to the orphanage. Nerline was staying with Miquette and her sister Sandra in Port au Prince. The baby got sick with leukemia in the orphanage and the orphanage called Nerline and told her the baby was too sick for other children and had to be taken back. Nerline said, "I can't take care of the baby," but the orphanage insisted. So she picked up the baby and took him to Sandra's home (now the original School of Hope building being leased by Sandra to TeacHaiti). Miquette was feeding the baby with a spoon but Nerline was alarmed that the baby wasn't eating, so she ran to get Miquette's mother. While she was gone, Miquette realized the baby in her arms had died and she laid the baby on a mat where he remained overnight. The next day, Nerline had to go out and purchase a simple little coffin and a burial lot to bury the baby.

When Nerline came to Port au Prince with the baby she left the abusive father. But her story is not untypical of what happens to young, uneducated girls—they have no place to go and end up in abusive relationships.

Nerline's children are now enrolled in the TeacHaiti School in St. Michel.

ANOUSE NORVILUS

Where will the next generation of Haitian doctors, engineers, lawyers and teachers come from? If Anouse Norvilus' dreams are realized, they will be her children and they'll stay in Haiti rather than move away.

Anouse grew up in St. Michel with Miquette, best friends from first grade through sixth, when Miquette moved away. They went to school and church together, were in programs together, sold fruit and kerosene (for home lamps) door to door together and even shared clothes and shoes with one another so each had twice as much to wear.

Anouse went through ninth grade herself and is now a street merchant selling sandals. She has three children, two in school, a seven year old son in a non-TeacHaiti school and an eleven year old sixth grade girl in an all-girls TeacHaiti School. Before she got her act together several years ago, the daughter's scholarship was suspended by Miquette because her grades weren't good enough. Anouse realizes how difficult that decision must have been for Miquette—suspending the daughter of her best friend, but she appreciates the courage to not compromise the program's standards.

From that point on, the daughter, Luanna, buckled down and now her mother says "she is the smartest girl in the class." She now has dreams of being a doctor, an ob-gyn who delivers babies. She believes that anything is possible for a kid from St. Michel, Miquette being a perfect example. Anouse hopes her son will become an engineer, lawyer or teacher.

Nothing Good Can Come Out of Nazareth

Anouse remembers a quote from the Bible to the effect that "Nothing good can come out of Nazareth." That is the way many locals thought about their own St. Michel. What would you expect from a city without electricity, water, sewer or grocery stores? They didn't expect anybody from their neighborhoods to achieve anything. A few from more prosperous neighborhoods accounted to something, but they never returned. But Miquette made it and she and Art have a modest home in Miquette's old neighborhood. It's the home Miquette grew up in—now fixed up.

CHAPTER 17

DETROIT LAKES BOARD AND SUPPORTERS

*"There is always one moment in childhood
when the door opens and lets the future in."*

—*Graham Green*

If the reader is to consider supporting the TeacHaiti mission, he or she should know who sits on the Detroit Lakes Board of Directors, who actively supports TeacHaiti, and what their backgrounds are.

The Chairman of the Board is Tom Klyve who has broad and varied experience as a paramedic, emergency service provider, entrepreneur, successful business owner, banker and chief financial officer. For the past 6 years he has been employed as Chief Financial Officer of SNAPS Holding Company, owner of Knight Printing Company and other entities. He has held a number of leadership positions in the community, organizations such as the Detroit Lakes School Board, Chamber of Commerce, Development Authority, St. Mary's Hospital Foundation, Becker Lakes Industrial Development Commission, and First Lutheran Church.

When Miquette graduated from Concordia and became a nurse, she worked at the Emmanuel Nursing Home where Klyve became acquainted with her. Being aware of Klyve's history of leadership, business background and solid judgment through Pastor Dave Peterson and others, she recruited him to assist in organizing a charitable non-profit organization to grant scholarships to poor students in Haiti. He assisted and TeacHaiti achieved IRS 501 (c)(3) tax status, ensuring that donations to TeacHaiti would be deductible for donors.

Klyve was immediately impressed with the personality and skills of Miquette. He saw how she instantly raised sufficient money to sponsor scholarships for 30 children in seven different schools, but negotiated fees and was able to place 41 children.

Klyve pondered how Miquette could place 41 children with funds for 30. He has been in Haiti twice, in August, 2010 and January, 2012, and has watched her operate. How does she persuade Haitian merchants to give discounts? How does she tell the story of TeacHaiti and gain financial support? Klyve notes her direct eye contact, her tone of voice, her body language and the voice of her convictions. The result is that people intervene to help her. Why do all the chips fall into place for her? It's not luck, says Klyve. People recognize something special in this person and in her passion. Not luck, but divine intervention. It's like Miquette was hand-picked by God for this mission.

Tom made his second trip to Haiti in January of 2012 with four other volunteers, including Dr. Clayton Jensen, Dr. Bill Henke, Nancy Henke and Denise Fredrickson. The main purpose of the trip was to work on the repair and finishing of the second building to be used as a TeacHaiti school. The building was just across the street (actually, more of a dusty trail) from the existing school. That building had previously been a small orphanage, but the orphanage couldn't pay the rent and they were out. The building had no water or electricity but Miquette made it a school.

But with two doctors along, the group set up a medical testing and screening operation described in the Clayton Jensen and Bill Henke interviews.

When the group arrived at the Port au Prince airport from their previous stop at Fort Lauderdale, they had 13 duffle bags each the size of hockey equipment bags. Six were filled with books from the Rossman Elementary School in Detroit Lakes for the teach-English curriculum, while four bags were filled with medical supplies, pharmaceuticals, etc., selected by Drs. Jensen and Henke, all donated by the Essentia Hospital and medical group at Detroit Lakes. The remaining bags carried luggage. Miquette had warned the Klyve group that medicine and medical supplies were absolutely illegal and would not be allowed by Haitian customs officials to enter the country. But she knew the group was planning to bring some, so she said "Don't get caught with medical supplies."

When the group got to customs, they were met by a uniformed 50 some-thing official with a badge and a gun. The official opened and inspected one bag that contained books. No problem. Then he opened a second bag of books. Again, no problem. Then he selected a third bag for inspection. Klyve knew this bag contained medical supplies because they were in a big box and the shape of the box was obvious through the zipped bag.

It happened that Miquette and her new husband Art had just returned from Ohio and were in the baggage claim area at the same time as the group from Detroit Lakes, so Miquette caught up with the group when they were at customs. Miquette and Art were supposed to have arrived two hours earlier, but their plane was delayed in Fort Lauderdale because of mechanical problems.

When the customs agent selected the third duffle for inspection, Klyve whispered to Miquette "This bag is filled with medical supplies." The agent unzipped the bag and found the big box sealed with plastic tape. He pulled out a knife to cut the tape to inspect the contents. Miquette reached forward and put her hand on the box. Then she looked directly at the agent and said (in Haitian Creole) "There may be some medical supplies in these boxes." The agent said "If I see medical supplies, I'll have to confiscate them." Miquette: "Then don't look in this box."

The agent grew quiet. He looked at the six people behind Miquette. Klyve reported that at this point Miquette's eyes were pleading for compassion as she kept her hand firmly on the box. Agent: "Where is this going?" Miquette: "To the TeacHaiti School of Hope." Agent: "Is that the school that teaches kids in the poor part of town?" Miquette: "Yes." Agent: "I've heard of that school," then he looked at the team and said, "Get out of here," and he motioned the group to get out and load up. The group picked up their bags, loaded them on a trolley and got out.

Tom Klyve made this observation: "If Miquette had not been there, the medical supplies would have been confiscated and trouble would have followed. Miquette spoke the language and she had the nerve to challenge the agent. Nobody else could have done that." Then Klyve asks this question: "Was the two hour delay that brought Miquette to the scene when her presence was essential a coincidence, an accident, or again, was it divine intervention?"

Klyve is a strong supporter of teaching English to Haitian children beginning in the first grade. He notes there are many foreign companies, profit and non-profit, operating in Haiti, and all speak their native language and English. Any young adult who can read, write and speak English is well positioned to obtain a job in one of those foreign national offices and have a lifetime income. One of the objects of a TeacHaiti education is to raise each student out of illiteracy and poverty and make them self-sustaining. Beyond a high school education, TeacHaiti is now sponsoring fifteen college and vocational students. These students will be expected to be fluent in English and French in addition to their native Creole, and possibly other languages and equipped to pursue careers in occupations like nursing, medical lab, medicine, civil engineering and auto repair.

Some of Klyve's observations in his two trips to Haiti are quite vivid. He saw men clearing out demolition sites pushing wheelbarrows with flat tires rolling on steel rims. He saw that most streets have ruts and potholes that looked like bomb craters. He saw broken electrical lines hanging over streets, vines growing over the lines, broken power poles neglected so long the pole ends were starting to rot. The result was off-and-on electricity. He saw young kids drenched in sweat, pulverizing concrete blocks with hammers—to be shoveled into the mix for new cement. He saw no bulldozers, just a few rubber tire trucks, just one dump truck and one track hoe (a truck with tank tracks with a back hoe mounted on the back).

He noted there is no mail service in Haiti, and many buildings without addresses. He was astonished by how food was handled in August with temperatures over 100 degrees: miles of street vendors like flea market merchants selling fruit, vegetables, bread and eggs without bags or refrigeration. He saw children chewing on four inch sticks of sugar cane for a treat. They chew until the pulp gets rubbery, then they spit it out.

MARY LEE

The vice chair of the TeacHaiti board is Mary Lee. You have already read about her extensively in this book.

VICKI MARTHALER

The Financial Secretary of the Board is Vicki Marthaler who has been Chaplain of the Emmanuel Nursing Home (now Ecumen) since 1995. Her previous employment included five years in accounting and 16 years as Executive Director of the Lakes Area Building Association. She earned a bachelor's degree in secondary education and social studies in 1990 at the age of 40. She was a social studies teacher from 1990-1995 in the Alternative Learning Program in the Detroit Lakes Public Schools. She then completed studies in Clinical Pastoral Education and was certified by the Evangelical Lutheran Church of America (ELCA) as an Associate in Ministry before she was called to the Emmanuel Homes as chaplain.

Marthaler became acquainted with Miquette when Miquette worked at Emmanuel after she got her nursing degree. Miquette urged the chaplain to be on her new TeacHaiti board as it was being organized in 2006.

The earthquake of 2010 shook loose many additional dollars for the mission. Presently, through Miquette's connections and appearances, support is coming from Virginia, Pennsylvania, Texas, California, Vermont, Ohio (Art's home state), from Detroit Lakes, Fargo-Moorhead and from various churches and the Detroit Lakes Rotary and Kiwanis Clubs.

The donors are big and little, young and old. One 7 year old Sunday school girl named Kira brought a baggie full of coins she had saved totaling $5.82—enough to provide one school lunch per day for a Haitian child for a week. One resident of Emmanuel, an 86 year old widow named Ruby, learned of a fundraising event to be held at Emmanuel where folks were asked to donate $20 each. Ruby had become acquainted with Miquette when Miquette had worked as a nurse there. Ruby couldn't afford the ticket for the fundraiser, but she said "I want to be a part of this," and wrote a check for $5. She was invited to the fundraiser and attended.

TeacHaiti regularly gets checks from old folks in Detroit Lakes and Mahnomen, Minnesota of $10-$25 each year as memorials or in honor of birthdays or anniversaries of family and friends. These gifts are used as general funds.

Marthaler believes the largest single individual gift must have been directed by God. In June of 2011, a grandfather, not a member of First Lutheran in Detroit Lakes, attended an outdoor service at First Lutheran for the purpose of seeing a performance by his grandchildren who had just finished Vacation Bible School at the church. That happened to be the day Miquette spoke at the service, explaining the need, the hope, the dreams and the program for educating poor children in Haiti. The man, moved by her message, sent a check for $50,000 the next day. He was invited to meet Miquette. He said no thanks, the purpose of the gift was not to be personally recognized, but simply to help someone fulfill God's mission, and asked that he remain anonymous. That $50,000 is in the capital fund.

The books of TeacHaiti show three designated funds, general funds, scholarship funds and capital funds. The general fund is for general operating expenses of the School of Hope like teacher and staff salaries, postage, teaching supplies, office supplies, insurance, diesel fuel, water, transportation expenses, building repair and maintenance. The scholarship funds, of course, are for scholarships, including the students at the School of Hope. Capital funds, are being held for future expansions—land and buildings.

DENISE FREDRICKSON

Board member and treasurer, Denise Fredrickson has been in the banking business for 30 plus years and is presently Vice President of Mortgage Lending at the Midwest Bank of Detroit Lakes. Although it has not been specifically assigned for her to do so, much of her effort on the board has been focused on the sale of Haitian jewelry.

One School of Hope program is an art/craft exercise for the children and a fundraiser at the same time. The children make jewelry from colorful cereal boxes. The paper is compacted in such a way that the resulting beads, marbles and ceramics look like authentic, solid jewelry and are quite colorful and attractive. The cereal boxes are packed in old boxes and suitcases and brought into Haiti by missionaries, volunteer and visitors. Why don't the cereal boxes come from Haiti? Because processed cereal in Haiti is most expensive and would be a huge luxury for the poor children at the School of Hope. A box of cereal would cost the equivalent of $8 to $10, and as a result—it doesn't happen. There aren't any. The result is very attractive bracelets, necklaces, earrings and pins, sold in the U.S. at TeacHaiti fundraising events. The proceeds are used to pay tuition for TeacHaiti graduates pursuing trade school, college, or professional training.

Late in October, 2012, Miquette flew up from Haiti and met with Denise at an international exhibit in Minneapolis where TeacHaiti jewelry was on display and sold wholesale at a booth. Miquette and Denise gathered names of possible retailers and networked at the conference.

Denise took a work trip to Haiti in January, 2012 with a TeacHaiti group where she assisted as a painter at the school and "pseudo nurse" with the medical exams being conducted by Dr. Henke and Dr. Jensen described below. Sometimes she shared the personal snacks she had brought along with the people patiently waiting to see the doctor.

Denise remembers one street scene observed when she was riding to work in a pickup box: a motorcycle with two people, two turkeys, one duck and a handful of chickens—all in the grip of the passengers.

Denise also visited folks living in the School of Hope neighborhood. Leaning against the original school was a one room shelter of tin and cardboard without running water or a toilet where a 26 year old mother of five kids lived. How do they survive? The group visited a hospital across the street from the destroyed Presidential Palace, where Denise's most powerful memory was the smell of urine.

During her visit in the School of Hope, Denise became aware of a single finger scratching on her back. She turned around and found a little girl, eight or nine years old, who showed big eyes and open arms for a hug of welcome and gratitude.

Denise and her husband are sponsors of a post high-school student named Stefan who showed up at the School of Hope one day and said he would do anything they wanted if he could have one meal a day provided for students. Stefan was doing his best to separate himself from his companions who were drifting toward the street gang scene. It turns out he was artistic talent and is attending TeacHaiti art classes on Saturdays.

There are three accounts in Haiti, a dollar account, a local currency account, and a ministry account. The ministry account is earmarked for scholarships for TeacHaiti graduates. A bookkeeper is employed in Haiti. Teachers are paid using checks and government taxes are paid using business and certified checks.

Because of the increasing demands on Miquette's time, she has been employed as of the summer of 2012 as a half time employee of TeacHaiti.

Each $350 student scholarship covers tuition, books, two uniform t-shirts, a backpack and one meal daily. The tuition will also cover medical emergencies for the children. When the School of Hope was opened, grades 1-4 were enrolled. The next year, kindergarten was added. Then in the 3rd year, 2012-2013, 5th and 6th graders were included.

Other board member are Rhys Anderson, Monique Anderson and Steve Carlson.

DR. CLAYTON JENSEN

Clayton Jensen is a retired physician with an impressive resume. He spent his first two years of medical school at the University of North Dakota in Grand Forks. He received his M.D. degree from the Wake Forest School of Medicine in Winston Salem, North Carolina in 1958. He interned in the U.S. Public Health Hospital in Baltimore, Md. He was invited back to U.N.D. where he served as Associate Professor of Family Medicine in 1957-60. Then he practiced Family Medicine in Valley City, N.D. for 25 years (1960-1985). Then back to U.N.D., where Dr. Jensen was Chair of the Department of Family Medicine from 1985-1995. For those last two years (1993-1995) he was Interim Dean of the Medical School. He retired in 1995. His wife, Gloria, died in 1998, and he moved to Detroit Lakes in 2000.

Dr. Jensen went to Haiti as a volunteer in January, 2012, along with Dr. Bill Henke, Nancy Henke, Denise Frederickson and Tom Klyve. Jensen was expecting to be painting in the TeacHaiti School, which everybody did the first day. But the group carried hockey bags loaded with school books and supplies, and at least one of the bags had medicine and medical supplies.

The next day, the group attended a church service. The service was held in the auditorium of Miquette's school, the Quesqueya Christian School and was, according to Jensen, "an old time revival/gospel meeting." There was lots of enthusiasm and energy—not the kind of service Jensen was accustomed to growing up Lutheran. He loved it.

The following day was a tour of Port au Prince. Jensen noted the earthquake damage to the National Palace and hospital, but that was not nearly as dramatic as the damage to homes—block houses smashed, collapsing and cascading down the hills. The huge tent cities were most depressing. Deep trenches in the area of these cities were used as bathroom facilities. He saw children, street children, begging in the area of the National Palace. He could see how poor the Haitian people were— "They had nothing, but they were so beautiful and gracious."

Jensen saw a local taxi—called a "tap tap" —a pickup with an enclosed box and extra mattress on the floor for more passengers—that was so loaded, the front tires were rising from the ground and the vehicle couldn't be steered. Two passengers had to get off so the tap tap could balance and continue.

Dr. Jensen and Dr. Henke set up shop to examine and establish baselines for TeacHaiti students, with only one stethoscope and one ophthalmic scope (for looking into eyes and ears) between them. They recorded and charted the age, height and weight of each child. The looked into their eyes and ears and checked their noses, throats, teeth, hearts and lungs. They checked hair—looking for "nits" —parasites. When they found any, they had a special shampoo to chase them out.

The children were generally in good health, though about 50% had worms. This was determined, not by checking their stool, but by asking about areas of pain. Those who pointed to their stomachs had worms. The doctors had special worming medications and tablets to flush the worms. A permanent medical record was established for each student. Miquette, of course, is a nurse and will be in position to monitor the children. A mini-pharmacy was set up for dispensing medications under her supervision.

Before long, word got out and parents and other neighborhood adults started showing up to see the doctors. No serious pathology showed up with the exception of one elderly woman, possibly in her 80's who was desperately ill. She was poorly responsive, coughing up green phlegm and frothing at the mouth. She was probably terminal. She was immediately sent to a hospital for treatment.

Nancy Henke, Denise Frederickson and Tom Klyve were the first stop for the children in their medical profiling. Denise reported that she was serving as a "pseudo-nurse." They recorded the height, weight, age and blood pressure of each child then passed the kids along to Dr. Jensen and Dr. Henke. All five were wearing blue "medical scrub" outfits.

Of course it is essential that children have adequate hearing and vision in order to learn in the classroom. The group had no medical devices for testing hearing and vision, but they tested anyway. For hearing, they made clicks and finger snaps to determine if the children could hear. No problem in that area. Dr. Jensen said he'd like to buy an audiometer, a portable device for testing hearing, and return to Haiti another time to do the job right. For vision, the doctors created their own charts with Es of various sizes and in various formations to have the children tell which direction they saw the lines pointing. All this was done through two Haitian interpreters, both proficient in English and Haitian Creole and both intending to later go into medicine.

DR. BILL HENKE AND NANCY HENKE

Dr. Bill Henke, Detroit Lakes physician, and his wife, Nancy Henke, a graduate medical technician with a master's in Health Care Management, were members of the volunteer team working at the TeacHaiti School of Hope in January, 2012. Their immediate reaction was one of dismay at the minimal medical infrastructure in Haiti—lack of potable water, community health programs, public health clinics and clean modern hospitals. They noted that stream beds were garbage dumps—pits with pigs and goats scavenging for scraps of food. These streams are sources of drinking water—the source of health. It appeared that the basics of good health in Haiti were available only to those with means.

An Oasis Of Hope

The Henkes spent a day of cleaning and painting the newest unit of the School of Hope under construction, just across the street from the original unit. They were impressed by the school for what it already was and what it could be. Dr. Henke called the school "an oasis of hope in a vast desert of hopelessness." He felt the school had the potential to provide genuine structure to the neighborhood and the children growing up there. His concept of that structure was that the school should include a small clinic as a headquarters for health care and health education. The neighborhood could maintain the clinic with physicians and medical professionals rotating in and out as needed. The basic principles of good health would be taught, drilled and practiced: immunization, antibiotics, clean water, proper diet, public and private hygiene, pregnancy planning, triage, regular exercise, general preventive medicine, and regular checkups.

The group brought in twelve hockey bags full of donated medical supplies as well as medical books and school books, including school books in French from generous folks in Quebec.

Then the volunteers began to catalog and examine the children as described by Dr. Jensen. The children were all excited and all wearing their very best clothes for the occasion. In the process, the kids learned the American variations of the "high five" from Tom Klyve: high, low, too low (oops, missed—too slow). Soon, word got around the neighborhood and parents and neighbors showed up wanting to be examined. There was no electricity in the work area, so examination had to cease at sundown. But, long lines were forming, so cut-offs had to be established. Once, it was announced that nobody standing behind a lady in a rose dress could be seen that day. But the folks kept coming. When the line was checked, it turned out the lady in the rose dress was allowing scores of parents to go forward from behind her to the front of the line.

Meeting and serving the children, their parents and the neighbors was very emotional. The children and adults were so appealing—open, friendly, smiling and appreciative. The need is obviously huge and the result is that caring hearts go out to the kids and their families. The work felt good—it felt right. What the volunteers discovered is that the people of Haiti get into your heart. One senses that Bill and Nancy Henke are quite likely to serve there again.

JEFF NORBY

Jeff Norby, a former TeacHaiti board member has made five trips to Haiti as of the date of this book. He is almost certain to make more. The first trip was a joint graduation gift. In January, 2007, Jeff and his daughter Annie both graduated from the University of North Dakota at the same time. Jeff walked across the stage first with a Bachelor's Degree from the College of Liberal Arts. Annie followed with a degree in paralegal studies.

On Easter of that year there was a family get-together at the Norby home to meet the family of their daughter Erin's husband, Peter Thiele. One of Peter's family members was his sister, Joanna Thiele. Joanna was a nurse who filled the family with details (and inspiration as it turned out) about her numerous trips to Haiti to do bricks and mortar work at an orphanage. Joanna told them she was going again—she was leading a group of young adults from the Twin Cities. Jeff and Annie listened and agreed to go—a joint graduation gift.

Jeff had been in Honduras earlier on a vacation trip. While there, he observed an area of extreme poverty—tin huts, miserable living conditions and hunger. He told himself, "Something is wrong with this picture." The seeds of the desire to return and do something were planted.

So in August of 2007, Jeff and Annie joined Joanna's group of about 20 volunteers and did brick and mortar work on a clinic and orphanage. While there, Joanna introduced Jeff and Annie to a woman (Mary, a social worker from Indianapolis) at the guest house who was in Haiti for a six month stint working with Mother Theresa's Sisters of Charity. She spoke the Creole language, necessary to communicate in Haiti. Two days a week, Mary walked 1 ½ miles to downtown Port au Prince, to work at a "wound clinic." She asked Jeff and Annie to go along.

The wound clinic was a walk-in program where long lines of people waited to have their wounds treated, all by volunteers. There were wounds and more: people had been hit by autos, had bike accidents, heavy infected broken bones and malnutrition. Some bore wounds like Jeff had never seen before. He removed one dirty bandage and found a gaping wound all the way to the bone. One woman had a big boil of infection over her breast. There were no doctors working that day, but one capable woman with on-the-job training decided the boil had to be lanced. Jeff held one arm, Annie held the other, and the lance was done. The woman screamed and a stream of pus shot six feet into the air. Jeff and Annie unwrapped old bandages, applied salve and anti-bacterial applications, changed dressings and worked with this endless wounded mass of humanity in separate languages and felt immense appreciation and fulfillment. Jeff called this the most intense experience of his life. They worked there two days, more mentally prepared the second day. But the experience remained so intense and they were so busy that it could not be processed until later.

Jeff and Annie also worked at Mother Theresa's Home for the Dying. They did AIDS testing with finger prick then applied the blood to a strip that indicated, like a litmus test, by color, whether or not the patient was positive. Those being tested were mostly in their 20s and about nine out of ten tested positive. Jeff was working in the men's ward, Annie in the women's ward and the results of the tests in the women's ward were about the same.

Jeff was asked many times if he was a doctor. He is actually a soil conservation technician working for the U.S. Department of Agriculture, doing natural resource conservation work. Annie is a paralegal. Jeff and Annie also gave back and foot massages in the same ward. Jeff felt the benefits were way beyond the purely physical benefits—the value of a human touch.

Also, with other members of Joanna's group, Jeff and Annie worked at the Sisters of Charity Children's Hospital. All they did was hold babies—tiny babies, just to have someone touch them. He felt the babies were starved for the human touch and they just clinged to the volunteers.

Look Out, These Kids Will Pick Your Pockets

They also worked at the orphanage where they were warned "Look out, those kids will pick your pockets." Mary was giving Jeff and Annie a tour to show the multiple needs for helping hands in Haiti.

They met nuns from France, India and the U.S.A. who had worked elsewhere but wanted to return to Haiti to work with the poorest of the poor. Jeff was impressed by the street-smarts, twinkle and mischievous sense of humor of the nuns, not to mention their obvious commitment and dedication. They seemed more motivated by pure love and caring rather than some programmed mission.

This trip was in August. The bricks and mortar work was done at 118° and the humidity had to be around 100%. Jeff noted that the Haitians they were working with rarely paused for a break or drink of water.

Back in the United States, Mary Lee, a member of the TeacHaiti board, learned about Jeff's trip to Haiti and Jeff was invited to become a member of the board. He had met Miquette and was familiar with the mission so he eagerly joined the board. He served as a board member for 5 years.

Miquette was still living in Detroit Lakes in 2007, working as a nurse at St. Mary's Hospital. She was contacted by Joanna Thiele who read about her in a newspaper and they became close friends. Both Miquette and Joanna were in Port au Prince during the earthquake on January 12, 2010. While Miquette was searching for her students, Joanna was searching for Miquette. All were safe, but Joanna was traumatized by the shaking earth.

Jeff Norby's second trip to Haiti, before the earthquake, was a solo effort, partly to represent TeacHaiti and partly to establish contacts to see if he could use his soils background in any beneficial way. Jeff had developed a contact list on his first trip and intended to follow up. On his first trip, he had met Gertrude Bienamie who was running an orphanage, Children's Hospital and guest house. Gertrude knew Jeff was coming again so she said she'd send Patrick to pick him up at the airport.

Jeff was carrying $2,000 in cash that he had collected in Detroit Lakes for TeacHaiti and Gertrude's orphanage. When Jeff arrived at the airport there was great confusion with people grabbing passenger bags to pull them to their waiting taxis. Patrick was supposed to identify himself with a sign: Provident Guest House. A young man approached Jeff and Jeff asked "Are you Patrick?" The young man hugged Jeff and said "Yes, come with me." Jeff gave him the address of his destination (the Providence Guest House) and they hit the streets. It soon became obvious the guy didn't know the way. Jeff realized he wasn't Patrick.

Along the way, the driver was stopped at a police check point. The police were armed with AK-47s. They checked "Patrick's" license. Then the police directed Jeff to get out of the vehicle. They searched his suitcase, finding clothes and nursing supplies. Then the police pointed to Jeff's duffle bag with the cash inside. The cash was in an envelope on the bottom. Jeff was terrified. The police gave a glance at the stuff on top and waved him through. The police could have grabbed a handful of cash or found some reason to detain him and extract some "release" funds. Close call, and he still had "Patrick" to deal with. Well, Patrick did charge an outrageous fee, but he eventually got Jeff to the Guest House after a long ride.

Jeff met with Miquette and her TeacHaiti scholarship students at their modest schools. Then he spoke at a gathering of parents with Miquette providing interpretation. Jeff, a former Division I hockey player (years before his actual graduation with Annie), does not feel public speaking is among his gifts. He feels more effective in one-on-one relationships. Nevertheless the appearance of a volunteer had to be encouraging and beneficial. While he was there he was back at the Children's Hospital and Orphanage—holding babies again.

The agricultural aspect of the trip did not turn out. Jeff had envisioned the possibility of taking soil samples back to the U.S. for analysis to establish micro-loans for peanut farmers. The University of Minnesota and the U.S.D.A. had been alerted and were ready to cooperate. Miquette directed him to the farms where he took soil samples to be tested for fertility, but U.S. authorities would not permit Haitian soil to be taken into the country. Accordingly, the ag mission was abandoned.

Jeff remembers the smells of Haiti: the food of street vendors and the stench of open sewers as he walked about.

Jeff made his third trip to Haiti in August of 2010. His group consisted of his daughters, Annie and Gretchen, TeacHaiti President, Tom Klyve,

Melissa Bergman, a teacher from Hoffman, Minnesota and the author of this book. The main purpose of this trip was to paint the house TeacHaiti had leased for its own school. The group stayed in the Heartline Ministries Guest House, available at low rates to groups and individuals doing volunteer "mission" work in Haiti.

While at the Heartline Guest House, Norby overheard a conversation involving Pastor John McCool, President of Heartline, about a special tour and meeting scheduled the next day in the Citè Soleil section of Port au Prince, and asked Pastor McCool if he could accompany the Heartline group and was invited to come along.

The Citè Soleil is an extremely impoverished and densely populated commune in Port au Prince that originally developed as a shanty town and grew to a population of 200,000-400,000 people. The area is one of the biggest slums on the Western Hemisphere and one of the most dangerous. The area has virtually no sewers, but has a poorly maintained canal system for the same purpose. The area was largely ruled by a number of gangs, each controlling their own sectors, until about 2007, when the United Nations stabilization mission in Haiti reestablished a degree of shaky government control.

The area was originally designed to house sugar workers, but developed into a magnet for squatters and laborers from around the countryside looking for factory work. Half the houses are made from cement with a metal roof and half are made entirely with scavenged material. Norby saw tin buildings that all seemed to be connected with only the narrowest of pathways between sections. He said it looked like an easy place to get lost, and if ever kidnapped, brought there and never found.

Though the gangs no longer rule the area, murder, rape, kidnapping, looting and shootings are still common. The area has been referred to as a microcosm of all the ills in Haitian society: endemic unemployment, illiteracy, absence of public services, unsanitary conditions, raw poverty, crime and armed violence. Norby says the United Nations has listed the Citè Soleil ghetto as one of the top five most dangerous places in the world.

Pastor McCool has worked among the poor of Haiti for many years and is well known to the gangs. McCool apparently had some money at his disposal to sponsor educational scholarship programs for Haitian children— not unlike TeacHaiti. A meeting had been arranged to meet with a gang about educating kids in Citè Soleil.

The meeting was held in the upstairs of a two story shack in the slum. Four or five gang members were there and about four Heartline members. Before sitting down to talk, the men all shook hands. Norby had been warned that the required method (by necessity) for shaking hands is to first hold out both hands, palms up, to show there are no hidden weapons. As the men talked, one gang member put on surgical gloves and kept rolling the sleeves up and down. Norby didn't understand the meaning of that riveting habit, but it seemed threatening to him and made him very nervous.

They talked through an interpreter. The gang people wanted to start their own school and basically wanted the Heartline money turned over to them. Heartline did not intend to fork it over, so they said no way. The discussions were heated enough to make Norby quite uneasy. But, McCool was careful not to let the rhetoric get out of hand. It was clear from what Norby heard that the gangs respected McCool. They conceded that when he said he would do something in the past, he kept his word.

The discussion lasted about an hour and a half. While the talking was taking place, there was the sound of a huge commotion below. It sounded like a fight had broken out. Norby thought a mob was forming outside. Several gang members left the meeting to see what was happening. Back upstairs, they explained that whenever white people came into their streets it was assumed they had money for something. They were upset that they weren't in on the talks. Who was going to get money and who was going to be shut out?

After the talks, the gang gave the group a tour of their area. Norby got the idea that there were two main gangs in the Citè and their territories were divided by a huge sewage canal. The Heartline group never talked to the gang on the other side of the canal. He said what he saw was "beyond words," scary and heartbreaking—a disaster area, but not because of the earthquake. He would never go there without security and never allow any member of his family (wife, three daughters) to go under any circumstances.

Norby was told that when the earthquake of 2010 destroyed buildings, it also wrecked prisons and prisoners escaped. Many found their way (back maybe) to Citè Soleil and disappeared.

Norby went along with TeacHaiti President, Tom Klyve, on another side trip while in Haiti. They had discussions about the possibilities of cooperative efforts with another ministry group, this one providing medical services. The doors were left open to some partnership projects, but nothing ever came of it and Jeff believes this other group is not presently operating in Haiti.

On this third trip to Haiti, the TeacHaiti group visited an orphanage operated by Gertrude Bienamie. Jeff and the group members had the impression that the orphanage had an unusually high number of children with special needs. Apparently numbers of children are simply "dumped" at the doorstep of the home and abandoned, including many newborns with obvious handicaps, physical and developmental. The children crave the attention they get from visiting strangers and enjoy the little games and teasing that takes place. Those who are infants and developmentally disabled needed assistance to be fed and the visitors were put to work helping out. The feeding time, because of the pitiful condition of the children and the mush being fed to them, was an emotional and heartbreaking exercise for the visiting volunteers. Gertrude begs and accepts help from wherever she can get it for her orphanage. She will room next door to Mother Theresa someday.

Gertrude is all over the place, really. The first two times Jeff Norby was in Haiti, he stayed at the Providence Guest House, run by Gertrude. She employs cooks and housekeepers and temporarily houses volunteers going to work at the Children's Hospital and orphanage—a separate organization operated by the Sisters of Charity. Gertrude worked hand in hand with the Sisters and went to church with them. But the Providence Guest House was destroyed by the earthquake and has not been rebuilt to date.

Norby has felt his life enriched by watching Miquette work toward the education of the children of Haiti. Jeff's own personal priority, perhaps as the father of three daughters, is the education of young Haitian girls. Young girls, in developing countries around the world, are oppressed, exploited, enslaved and abused. Worldwide they are the downtrodden of the downtrodden. When girls become literate, they have taken the first step toward self-respect, independence and freedom from oppression. Birth rates go down and equality with men becomes closer to possible.

After the earthquake, Norby's employer the U.S. Dept. of Agriculture, Natural Resources Conservation Services, advertised for applications for a position to be developed in Haiti for a 6 to 12 month project—details not spelled out, but probably a conservation or environmental project. With the support of his wife, Michelle, Jeff applied for the job. He would have loved the opportunity to help in a country on the verge of environmental collapse (deforestation, erosion, etc.). But, after reconsideration, our government dropped the idea for two reasons: the government in Haiti was too unstable and budgetary considerations.

MICHELLE NORBY

Michelle Norby is a graduate medical tech with a degree in clinical laboratory science. She is married to Jeff Norby.

When the earthquake hit Haiti in January of 2010, Michelle felt called to go and help. She joined a team of about 10 medical people from Detroit Lakes, including a French Canadian orthopaedic surgeon, Dr. Cormier, who could speak French. He was one of the four medical people helping who could speak a language that many Haitians understood and he delighted in using his native tongue.

The group arrived in mid-February, but they couldn't fly into Haiti because the Port au Prince airport was damaged and unable to handle traffic, so they had to land in the Dominican Republic. They needed to rent ground transportation to get to Haiti. But—not so fast. Before they could cross the border to get into Haiti they were taken to an international "no man's land," a space between two fences, one leaving the Dominican Republic and one entering Haiti. There they waited.

In order to take medical supplies into Haiti, they had to bribe the border security people with cash and medical supplies ("my mother really needs an inhaler"). Can you imagine having to pay bribes to come and help the people you are bribing?

But still they were stalled in "no man's land." Finally, a man in the zone, not an official, said "what are you doing here?" They explained that they were going to meet with Miquette who was to coordinate and direct their medical offerings. "Miquette? Miquette?" He asked "I know Miquette." With that, he called Miquette, verified their story, and arranged their entry across the Haitian border and led them all the way to the gates of the Quisqueya Christian School in Port au Prince, the medical coordination center and staging site. They never did learn just exactly who this guy was. From the time they landed in the Dominican Republic, it took them about eight hours to travel the less than 154 miles to get to their destination in Haiti.

The medical crew slept in tents on the soccer field at the Quisqueya coordination center. They stayed there for 12 days. The level of coordination, directed by Miquette was amazing. The volunteers were organized into medical teams. Every evening there was a meeting with teams told where to go in the city with their particular expertise. Art McMahon, later to become Miquette's husband, coordinated the transportation. The teams drove to their destinations in pickup and truck boxes bouncing over unbelievably rough streets, "hanging on for dear life." The smell of human flesh was in their noses as they trucked to their assignments, passing piles of rubble and rock.

One assignment was to one of the better hospitals in Port au Prince. This is where the well-off people from the city went. Actor Sean Penn was keeping this hospital open by providing generators and gas for electricity. This became the center for orthopedic care and surgery. The hospital was open, but heavily damaged and not safe. Surgery was done inside in the operating room, but the patients were then immediately wheeled into the outdoor courtyard down below to heal. They were attended to on cots in open canvas shelters on the ground.

The teams worked at various temporary "medical centers" around the city. They were tent cities, but the shelters weren't really tents, they were sticks or poles holding up tarps or sheets. They had no running water and no sanitation. One of the largest centers was just across the street from the destroyed presidential palace and it was the only one with port-a-potties, but they were never emptied—almost making them more gross than none at all.

When the medics arrived at the tent city care centers, people were lined up waiting for medical care. Included were mothers carrying newborn babies that had never been seen by a doctor or nurse before. Who delivered the babies and where? Norby did a little of everything that could be done with her basic medical knowledge. She helped triage patients, acted as a pharmacist, took blood pressure and pulses and even did some physical therapy. But she had no laboratory and no instruments that worked, so she found herself guessing about hemoglobin counts.

Under every patient's mattress was his or her dossier—medical results printed in multiple languages, because every week some new medical team would be attending to them. Some patients kept the dossier under their pillows.

Norby remembers one woman patient who said her tears couldn't come out of her eyes so they were coming out of her chest. The traumatized woman not only had scabies on her chest, she was probably experiencing post-traumatic stress disorder, common not only among the injured, but the entire population. Examinations of the spongy tummies of the children revealed that many of them had internal parasites—worms that required medication.

The children and patients in general were fascinated by Norby's blue eyes. Most of them had never seen blue eyes before.

JOANNA DOLS

When Joanna Dols got married in 2012, wedding guests were directed to not give wedding gifts, but if they wished, to contribute to a clean water project being conducted by Healing Haiti. Joanna, a graduate of Concordia College in Moorhead, Minnesota has been working as a nurse in labor and delivery at the Park Nicollet Methodist Hospital in Minneapolis for the past 16 years.

In 2004, Nurse Dols decided she wanted to go on a foreign mission trip before she reached her 30th birthday. In April of 2005 she signed on with a group from Calvary Lutheran Church of Golden Valley, Minnesota for a trip to Haiti. The purpose of that trip was to help build a cinder block wall around an orphanage. Before the earthquake of January, 2010 she made seven more trips with different groups, almost always to do construction.

After her second mission trip, Dols and four friends organized a non-profit group called the Haiti Mission Project. The purpose, along with doing construction projects, was to build relationships with the Haitian people by asking questions, listening, understanding and helping wherever needed: making meals, watching children and odd jobs. "Everybody deserves to be validated and listened to, as well as shown respect and love, not pity," said Dols. But in addition, with her medical training and experience, she worked in an orphanage for children with special needs being operated by Gertrude Bienamie as well as a children's hospital and a home for the dying.

She was stunned at the level of poverty she saw and returned home to share what she had experienced. Her group did fundraising in Minnesota to raise money to make the trip to Haiti and to help support Gertrude's orphanage and a clean water project. The trips were made by groups of 6 to 18 people for periods of one week to 10 days.

Dols was obviously developing a passion for doing what she could in Haiti. Just before Thanksgiving, 2009, she left her job on a three month leave of absence and went to Haiti with a group that had 13-14 people in the beginning. The purpose of the leave was to work with Gertrude in her orphanage, work in the children's hospital, to work in pre-natal care, labor and delivery. The maternity work was done through Heartline Ministries directed by John McCool. During this period she was staying in a guesthouse operated by the same Gertrude Bienamie who operated the orphanage and children's hospital.

Jesus is Coming

The January 12, 2010 earthquake struck while Joanna was in Port au Prince. Fortunately, she was not in Gertrude's guest house because it was totally destroyed and she probably would have been killed. She was volunteering at the time as a midwife at the maternity center in the Heartline Clinic only three blocks away. When the quake struck, there was a horrible loud crash like a semi-truck being hit by a train. People were running outside from the buildings they were in. Haitians were screaming "Jesus is coming" in Creole. Joanna says the earthquake changed everything. Volunteers who wanted out were flown out in "cargo embassy" flights. Joanna elected to stay.

John McCool took charge of his Heartline Ministries volunteers. "This is a major earthquake," he said, "and it's bad." He instructed Joanna to take children from the neighborhood to his home, a sheltered place, and stay there until it was safe to come out.

Even before the dust settled, Heartline Ministries organized a two story cinder block building into a "MASH" unit for emergency medical care. They sent out trucks and brought injured victims in, 12-14 at a time, for medical attention, including surgery. Doctors with medical supplies, nurses and other volunteers were flown in to save lives and patch up the injured. For the last three weeks of January, Joanna managed a makeshift pharmacy in the unit. Meanwhile, in the streets and in the rubble, the search for victims went on and people were staggering about, crying and screaming. Eventually the smell led rescuers to the bodies of those who didn't make it.

One effect of the quake, not often mentioned, is the post-traumatic terror that haunted many who experienced the earthquake. Joanna was working on the second story of the clinic when the shaking started. She experienced about 50 seconds of panic while evacuating the building. Patients coming into the emergency unit were all giving their personal details—where they were, what happened and who they lost. They were stunned and dazed, and the impact didn't go away quickly. For many, it has continued ever since. This is post-traumatic stress disorder. Joanna herself engaged in therapy when she returned home and has largely recovered, but still has bad dreams. For most in Haiti there has been no therapy and no forgetting. Even "survivor guilt" remains for some.

John McCool appreciated the dedicated work of the volunteers who stayed. He saluted them with words from the fourth chapter of Esther: "You were meant for such a time as this."

Nurse Dols has made nine more trips to Haiti since the earthquake. She says she is committed to serving the people of Haiti for the rest of her life and will continue to go there at least once a year. Her husband went with her after they were married in 2012 and will probably go again every year.

The Ultimate Resource

Dols read about Miquette Denie and her mission in the Fargo Forum while she was visiting her aunt in Fargo. Since Dols and Miquette are both

Concordia graduates, both nurses, and both devoted to the people of Haiti, she had to meet her. Once she met her (no doubt gushing over one another's C-rings), she concluded that Miquette and her passion made her "the ultimate resource" because she understands the American culture and the Haitian culture. Even before the earthquake, Dols sponsored one child in a TeacHaiti School and has sponsored one every year since. She visited the child and her mother on one of her trips to Haiti. She has visited the School of Hope several times and has come away with the impression that the children really want to be there and their families will do anything to keep them there. She visited one annual Christmas party at the school and said it seemed weird to see Santa Claus when it was hot outside. She remains in regular contact with Miquette.

CHAPTER 18

HEALTH IN HAITI

*"He who has health has hope,
he who has hope has everything."*

—Arabian Proverb

Public Health in Haiti is bad news and good news. The bad news is what it has been and what it is now. The good news is, that unlike education, something is being done about it.

The bad news first. Since over 80 percent of the population live below the poverty line, malnutrition is a national anguish. Half the population is characterized as "food insecure." The physical symptoms are obvious: over half of all Haitian children are undersized. Twenty year old Miquette Denie weighed 105 pounds when she came to America.

The World Health Organization (WHO) estimates that only 43% of the population receives the recommended inoculations, which are surely needed since less than half of all Haitians have access to clean drinking water. Sanitation is even worse.

Of the nations in the Western Hemisphere, Haiti is last in per capita spending on health care with only $83.00 per person being spent each year. Why? For one reason, there are only 25 physicians and 11 nurses per 100,000 population. Another reason is that in many rural areas there is absolutely no access to health care. Only one fourth of births are attended by skilled medical professionals.

Haiti has the highest incidence of HIV/AIDS outside of Africa, thanks in part to the sex trade commerce initiated when Baby Doc was ruling and thanks in part to the inadequate health infrastructure. As a result, over 5,000 babies are born affected with the AIDS virus every year.

Mental health problems did not begin with the 2010 earthquake, but they got a severe jolt upward at that time. Before and since the quake, there was and still is a serious shortage of mental health professionals. The result is that among the poor and illiterate, people in distress turn to superstition and voodoo—getting about the same relief as a medical patient gets from a placebo.

Maternal and childcare needs go largely unattended. Of every live birth in Haiti, only one out of 1,000 is attended by a midwife and the risk of death for the mother is one in 93. After birth, the leading causes of infant deaths are diarrhoeal disease, intestinal infections, parinatal disease, malnutrition and parasitic diseases.

The good news is that a turnaround is taking place. The turnaround of health in Haiti is best told through the story of Paul Farmer. Farmer is an American physician who first went to Haiti as a student volunteer in 1983. He grew up in Alabama, living with his family in a bus and a fifty foot boat (without running water) when he graduated from high school. His family traveled about and never got a sense of hometown. He studied under a full scholarship at Duke University and lived among the privileged. But he quit his fraternity when he realized they were an "all-white" organization.

At Duke, Farmer studied medical anthropology and learned how, in the early 20th century in Upper Silesia, there was an epidemic called famine fever, now relapsing fever, a social upheaval caused by overcrowding, poor hygiene and malnutrition. This all made sense to him and he developed a moral understanding of public health. As a result, he got interested in migrant labor camps not far from the Duke campus in Raleigh, North Carolina. A Belgian nun, Julianna DeWolt, was working with Friends of the United Farm Workers, and through her he met a number of Haitian farm workers living in wretched conditions near the farm fields. He began reading everything he could find about Haiti. He protested against the American immigration policy that allowed entrance to most refugees from Cuba, but turned back fleeing Haitians to the cruelest most self-serving dictatorship in the Caribbean for more hunger and disease. He learned French and began studying Creole which he called a Romance language.

Farmer went to Haiti in 1987, intending to spend a year there. He had worked as a volunteer of the Duke University Hospital and had applied for admission to medical school at Harvard. Baby Doc Duvalier was still ruling over Haiti in 1983, still murdering political enemies, and still stealing and misappropriating foreign aid as his father, Papa Doc, had done.

He connected with a small charity called Eye Care Haiti in Port au Prince with outreach clinics in the countryside, so he headed for the countryside. He had $1000 in his pocket from a winning essay about Haitian artists, and figured he could make it on that since the average Haitian lived on less.

He Could Speak Creole Like A Rat

Within weeks, Farmer had quickly picked up an amazing grasp of the native language and was told that he could already speak Creole "like a rat." What Farmer found was most discouraging, but no surprise. Farmer traveled from place to place in Haiti, hitching rides on the back of pickup trucks or riding on tap-taps with the peasants, their chickens and their baskets of mangos. He came down with dysentery, probably because he ate food he bought on the streets. He came to know sick and discouraged people resigned to their poverty and illnesses. He discovered that what few hospitals there were, fees kept the poor from seeking help. He saw people ill because they didn't have the $15 needed for a blood transfusion. He said "I'm going to build my own (expletive) hospital and there will be none of that there, thank you."

They Died of Haiti

Farmer came upon a "wretched, dusty, squalid settlement named Cange. Cange was totally without—without a clinic, without a hospital and with-out a community health system. He decided Cange was where he would do something. He started by walking hut to hut through Cange and two neighboring villages and taking a preliminary health census of families, re-cent births and deaths and the apparent causes of morbidity and mortality. He found the mortality among infants and juveniles was "horrific" and that deaths of mothers were common. He was so discouraged by conditions, he said of some of the dead: "They died of Haiti."

But Farmer wasn't a doctor yet. He entered the Harvard Medical School in the fall of 1984 at the age of 24. He was registered as a full time student, but he attended classes only sporadically for the first two years. In between, he shot back and forth to Cange with medical books and supplies to bring medicine to people without doctors. Be he showed up for the lab practi-cums and exams and somehow managed to earn very good grades.

We're Just Helping Them Not To Go To Hell

Under the direction of a South Carolina Episcopal group and Pere Lafon-tant, who operated a one-doctor clinic in Mirbalais, not far from Cange, a small clinic was built in Cange. Farmer was there from the beginning. The clinic had one sink and electricity generated through solar power. The first microscope was stolen by Farmer from the Harvard Medical School. "Redistributive justice," he called it. "We were just helping them not to go to hell."

The Cange project was costing more than the Episcopalians had. Farmer connected with a construction millionaire from Boston, Tom White, and became his friend. Farmer impressed White with his commitment and persuaded him to part with millions over the years in the development of the Mirabalais clinic and other projects. Farmer said, "Lives of service depend on lives of support."

Haiti Burns Itself Into Your Brain

The story of Paul Farmer and his work in Haiti is a story of commitment, then passion, then (almost) obsession. He worked for years in Haiti with a tireless worker, Ophelia Dahl (who said "Haiti burns itself into your brain"). He loved her and she loved him and he asked her to marry him. She turned him down, but continued to work with him, because of his unswerving commitment and massive devotion to the poor. "The strain of living with someone who always had a mission that came ahead of going for walks, dinner for two and normal domestic relations would have been too much. Being his wife would have been no bargain. But to be his friend is simply wonderful." Later, Farmer married a Haitian woman. Truly, Paul Farmer's devotion to the poor of Haiti is an inspiration. His story through 2013 is told in full by Tracy Kidder in *Mountains Beyond Mountains*.

In 1987, Farmer, Ophelia Dahl, Tom White, Tom McCormack and Dr. Jim Yong Kim organized a non-profit named Partners in Health for the purpose of "bringing the benefits of modern medical science to those in need of them to serve as an antidote to despair." The idea was to prevent diseases before they occur to avoid the necessity of curing them.

Partners in Health took over the clinic at Cange. The little village of Cange seemed like the end of the earth—one of the poorest, most diseased, eroded and famished regions in Haiti. After Partners in Health took over, the clinic became known as Zanmi Lasante, which in Creole means Partners in Health. After it opened, its staff grew and seven doctors, not all fully competent (Haitian medical training is marginal), and the entire staff were Haitian. Eventually, Zanmi Lasante built schools, houses, communal sanitation and water systems throughout its patient area. It vaccinated all the children and had greatly reduced malnutrition and infant mortality. Local rules required that Zanmi Lasante charge patients user fees, roughly the equivalent of eighty American cents for a visit. Even that minimal fee kept some people away. But Farmer, the Medical Director, dictated that every patient had to pay eighty cents, except women, children, the destitute and anyone who was seriously ill. Farmer's rule was that no one could be turned away. He said "I feel ambivalent about selling my services in a world where some can't buy them." Patients came in passenger trucks, on foot and by donkey at great distance because the eighty cents made a difference.

Genius Grant

The money for Sanmi Lasante, most of it, came from Partners for Health, and much of that from Tom White. But along the way, Sanmi Lasante and Paul Farmer became well known both in Haiti and abroad. In 1993, Farmer was awarded a so-called genius grant from the MacArthur Foundation and a Conrad N. Hilton Humanitarian prize of $1.5 million. He gave it all to Partners in Health.

Today, Sanmi Lasante has grown into a 104 bed hospital with two operating rooms, adult and pediatric inpatient wards, an infectious disease center (the Tom White Center), an outpatient clinic, a women's health clinic, ophthalmology and general medicine clinics, a laboratory, a pharmaceutical warehouse, a Red Cross blood bank, radiographic services and a dozen schools.

Tracy Kidder says: "All too often international aid organizations weaken the societies they are supposed to help. Often they rely almost entirely on professionals from the world's wealthy countries, and they fail to make their projects indigenous. This all but guaranties that their projects will neither grow nor last. Partners in Health is different. The organization now has on the order of 6,500 employees. The overwhelming majority came from the impoverished countries where PIH is working. Fewer than 100 of the employees come from the United States."

The organization has 11 other sites on Haiti's Central Plateau and beyond. It is one of the largest non-governmental healthcare providers in Haiti, employing mostly Haitian people, including doctors, nurses and community health workers. There are now 1.2 million people in their service area.

After the earthquake, Zanmi Lasante provided care to thousands who fled from ruins of Port au Prince and established medical outposts at four camps in the crippled city. Zanmi Lasante also announced a three year, $125 million plan to help Haiti build back with the Stand With Haiti Plan. Before the quake, Partners in Health had planned to build a new community hospital in Mirbalais. But after the quake, the project was accelerated and by July, 2010, ground had been broken on a world class national referral hospital and teaching center. In October, 2012, construction was completed. The hospital opened in March of 2013 and serves 185,000 in the Mirbalais area and sees 500 patients daily in its ambulatory clinics. The hospital also provides high-quality education for Haitian nurses, medical students and resident physicians. Mental health and psychological services will be increased dramatically in the hospital, supported in part by a $1.5 million grant from Grand Challenged Canada.

Partners in Health are moving forward scientifically as well. They have procured the development of Haiti's first oral cholera vaccine which, when distributed and administered by the World Health Organization, should prevent the recurrence of another cholera epidemic.

Also, in collaboration with Abbott Laboratories, Partners in Health have created a process to produce Nourimanba, a peanut and vitamin food supplement for distribution to malnourished children, especially those with stunted growth. A production plant makes about 70 tons of the product for 10,000 children each year as a second plant is being built which will push capacity to more than 350 tons and 50,000 children. The first plant guarantees a market for 250 Haitian peanut farmers and the second will need 350 additional producers.

The Man Who Would Cure The World

As a result of his work, Paul Farmer has become famous as an American anthropologist and physician who is best known for his humanitarian work providing "first world" health care for "third world" people, beginning in Haiti. Tracy Kidder, in *Mountains Beyond Mountains*, called him "the man who would cure the world." He has become recognized as a leader and world authority on health among people who live in poverty.

When the earthquake struck, Farmer rushed back to Haiti and spent the entire summer of 2010 in relief efforts. He wrote a book, *Haiti After The Earthquake* in which he says:

> I wanted to put some punctuation on the experience of the quake. It was a very grim experience for a lot of us. It was for me anyway.

I've been working in Haiti for 28 years – I thought I'd sort of seen it. I've gone through a number of coups, the storms of 2008, I thought, you know, that I'd seen things as bad as they were going to get, and I was wrong. It was the most difficult experience I've gone through, I can say that, emotionally it was very wrenching. It was nightmarish.

Farmer graded the relief effort since the earthquake:

I would say for humanitarian relief, right after the quake, I'd give a pretty decent grade, like a B. For reconstruction, I'd day we're lucky at C-/D+. . . . But at two years after the quake, only 30% of the rubble had been cleared, and at the end of May, 2012, 634,000 people remained in temporary camps, down from a peak of 1.5 million people in the summer of 2010, when I lived there. . . . It feels terrible to go back there and see so many people living such squalor. At the same time, from what we can tell, it's half as many people in those circumstances then a year ago.

He cited the cholera epidemic as a reason that public-sector utilities like water systems need to be strengthened. "For public health and public education, trying to bypass the public sector is a big mistake.

Partners in Health are not alone in building public health services in Haiti. Many organizations, including Doctors Without Borders (DWB) are active there. DWB currently employs 2500 people in that country, 85 percent Haitians, and manage four hospitals (510 beds) in the quake area where they treated 23,000 cholera cases.

Slowly, public health is making a turnaround in Haiti, a big, dramatic turnaround. Unfortunately, public education is not. Will there ever be public schools in Haiti with programs that equal what TeacHaiti provides? That is unlikely to happen for a long, long time. Until that time, if it ever comes, TeacHaiti will play a vital role in educating the poor children in Haiti.

CHAPTER 19

WHY IS HAITI SO POOR?

*"Once poverty is gone, we will need to build museums
to display its horrors to future generations. They'll wonder
why poverty continued so long in human society—how
a few people could live in luxury while billions
dwelt in misery, desperation and despair."*

—*Muhammad Yunus*

In 1986, Bob Corbett, Director of People to People, wrote an essay titled "Why is Haiti so Poor?" which he reviewed in 1999 and left unchanged. 1986 was the year Baby Doc Duvalier left office and Rene Preval took over in one of Haiti's few known peaceful transfers of power in the 20th century. He reviewed the history of Haiti through the Baby Doc Years.

Corbett concluded that the ultimate causes of Haiti's misery are human greed and the lust for power going back to French Colonialism, the introduction of slaves, the United States occupation from 1915-1934 and the elite's protection of its wealth.

Haiti was called the Jewel of the Antilles, the richest colony in the world. It produced over 50% of the Gross National Product of France. France realized incredible fortune from Haiti, importing sugar, coffee, cocoa, tobacco, cotton and dye indigo.

What happened? This great productivity was the result of slave labor, the most brutal system in the Caribbean. The ultimate threat to an unproductive slave elsewhere was that he or she would be sold to Haiti. But slavery didn't end when the French were thrown out. Instead, the concept of forced cheap labor was passed along to the native Haitian elite—Haitians who had Haitian slaves. Then, mulattos, the children of white masters and black slaves, received freedom and took on the practices of white masters, including religion, language (French), education, culture, and of course, the ownership of slaves.

The international community, mostly slave owners themselves, objecting to the example of France freeing slaves, established a boycott of Haitian products, seriously damaging Haiti's long-term economic development.

France drove a hard bargain with the newly independent Haiti and demanded payment for lands taken from former slave owners. In 1838, Haiti agreed to a 150 million franc debt for these lands. The debt pulled the Haitian economy down for over 80 years and was not fully paid until 1922. But during the interim, Haiti paid 150 francs many times over in interest on the debt. This burden had a huge negative impact on the Haitian economy over that period of time.

Corbett argues that the occupation of Haiti by the U.S. Marines from 1915-1938 was a serious blow to Haitian independence and self-image. The Marines took control of the collection of taxes and forced the repeal of a provision of the 1804 constitution that provided foreigners could never own land in Haiti. However, education was left untouched by the Marines and schools remained French in language and structure.

The Marines left in 1934, but he U.S. presence in the economy and government affairs was well established and remained. Especially after 1946, the U.S., through strings attached to aid packages, gave oppressive governments what they needed to stay in power. These despots were friendly to U.S. military, propaganda and economic interests, so they were supported. Though not America's intent, the Haitian people suffered as a result.

Corbett points out that 3% of Haitian people are the elite, who have used their positions in government since 1804 to gather wealth and power for themselves. The rule of the Duvalier family, Papa Doc and Baby Doc, represented a dramatic example of how it worked: terror, beatings, killings, illegal detentions and forced exits to keep the masses in line while their political followers and friends manipulated the wealth into their own hands. The corruption was so well established that it could not be sidetracked.

One hundred percent of the Haitian people speak Creole as their mother tongue. Yet French is the official language of the country. All government business is carried on in French and the schools educate mainly in French. There is no social prestige to anyone who cannot speak French. Yet, only about 10% of the people can get along in French and less than 5% know French fluently. So the path to social, economic and intellectual development in Haiti is reserved for speakers of French.

One result of the Haitian language exclusion is a high national illiteracy rate. For the illiterate, ideas about personal health, birth control, employment opportunities, agricultural practices, economics, responsive government and the vast world of literate-available information are out of reach.

Why is Haiti so poor? One of the most obvious and critical reasons is that the system of education is a failure and a disgrace. This factor is covered in full in Chapter 11, Education in Haiti.

With illiteracy and ignorance so pervasive in Haiti, is it any wonder that the country has allowed its forests to be depleted and its topsoil to be eroded? Because the only fuel in Haiti is wood, people cook with charcoal and massive amounts of wood are consumed for fuel. For the past 200 years trees have been cut and not replanted. When the rainy season came, with pounding rains for four or five months, the soil washed down the mountains and into the Caribbean Sea.

Haiti is primarily an agricultural land, and yet is an importer of food. Ownership of the most productive agricultural land is in the hands of the few. They choose to plant for export and not for local consumption because that is where the money is. The field workers are so poorly paid, they can only afford little of the imported food—a vicious cycle.

Haiti will remain poor until the infrastructure, mostly neglected for generations, is rebuilt. Inadequate roads make shipping goods from the rural areas to the markets in Port au Prince expensive and risky. Further, electricity is unavailable except for a few. This impacts business, education and health care. The lack of potable water has an even more dramatic impact. Sewage systems are available to only the wealthy in Port au Prince. For the rest, outhouses or just the outdoors is where it all happens. During one ride with Miquette through the streets of Port au Prince, we all observed a man urinating against a wall. This was a routine observation for Miquette who quipped "for men, the whole world is a latrine." But in Haiti it is said that 80% of all disease is water bourne. Thus, the lack of sewers in Haiti is a serious health problem.

Why has the infrastructure been so long neglected? Because their leaders have ripped off the people. Many millions of dollars in foreign aid and charitable groups for infrastructure projects have been diverted to fend off coups, for other political purposes and much has been just plain stolen by government officials, their families, friends and coherts.
Eighty percent of Haitians live on less than $2 per day—this is especially

tragic because of the strong link between poverty and vulnerability to natural disasters. A study by the Belgian Centre for Research on the Epidemiology of Disasters compared the impact of natural disasters among the 10 richest countries to those of the 10 poorest countries over a 30 year period. The conclusion was that the average number of victims per 100,000 population in the rich countries was 36. In the poor countries the number was 2,879 for the same number of disasters.

Why? Developed countries have sturdier construction, better infrastructure, a more diversified economy, greater ability to respond to emergencies, better insurance programs and access to savings and credit.

Developing nations successfully implement economic reforms and participating in globalizations. Haiti has not. Haiti's economic policies and dysfunctional institutions have kept Haiti poor.

Visitors to Haiti experience dysfunction almost wherever they go. This author went to the men's room at the Port au Prince airport. The urinal did not flush. The water did not run at the first sink I went to. There was no soap at any sink. The paper towel dispenser was empty. The air hand dryer didn't work. Elsewhere in the city, piped water delivery, where it existed, was unreliable, so Haitians are seen everywhere carrying jugs. Electric service is sporadic, so those who can afford it rely on gas-powered generators, while some have to live without light or use kerosene lamps.

The rules, regulations and fees relating to the establishment and carrying on of business have forced most businesses to operate "off the record" or in a shadow economy. This hurts the potential for the creation of wealth.

Haiti has a dismal record in the use of foreign aid. What needs to be done is to implement market reforms and develop an infrastructure that will support growth and development managed by Haitians themselves and not foreign experts.

Bob Corbett says that from his own experience, he has come to the conclusion that huge numbers of Haitians suffer from "a self-defeating image of themselves." They have been labeled ignorant and illiterate and know that they are poor in a rich world. They speak Creole, but French is the language of power, success and social prestige in Haiti. They feel powerless and believe it's their own fault. This mind-set feeds into the country's cycle of misery.

There is one added dimension to poverty as Mother Teresa saw it:
> We sometimes think poverty is only being hungry, naked or homeless; The poverty of being unwanted, unloved or uncared for is the greatest poverty; We must start in our homes to remedy this kind of poverty.

The focus then of Mother Teresa, and of this book is: who cares?

CHAPTER 20

WHY EDUCATION?

"It seems as though there are never enough books."
—*John Steinbeck*

As this modest volume points out, there are many pressing problems in Haiti: poverty, unemployment, the economy, health care, government, justice, crime, transportation, infrastructure (roads, bridges, clean water and sanitation), environment, education and more.

So why does TeacHaiti focus on education? A journey of a thousand miles begins with a single step and TeacHaiti can't build highways, so it begins with the single step of opening doors for the development of young minds. Education, it believes, is the highway out of the Haitian state of despair. If over 50% of a nation's population is illiterate, how will conditions ever change? The solution must come from within. Haiti must develop its own informed citizens, its own entrepreneurs, doctors, nurses, economists, engineers, clergy, craftsmen, tradesmen, administrators, lawyers, scientists, agronomists, technicians, teachers, professors and politicians.

Can a person truly be free if he or she is ignorant? A recent report by Australia's Walk Free Foundation in October, 2013 indicated that 29.8 million people around the globe are modern day slaves. India has the largest number with an estimated 13.9 million people, but Haiti has the second highest percent in bondage with 2 percent. Modern slavery as defined in the report is human trafficking, forced labor, and slavery-like practices such as denial of freedom or control and exploitation of another person for profit, sex or the thrill of domination. Girls in particular are abused—mentally, sexually and physically. The Haitian's have a name for these slaves—they are called restaveks. With a population of 8.2 million, if 2 percent are considered modern day slaves, there are 164,000 slaves in Haiti today.

The route out of slavery is education. Harriet Beecher Stowe wrote the classic *Uncle Tom's Cabin* in 1852. She stated the problem of "freeing the slaves" in the words of Miss Ophelia a member of a slave owner's family:

> Perhaps it is impossible for a person who does no good not to do harm. But suppose we should rise up tomorrow and emancipate, who would educate these millions and teach them how to use their freedom? They would never rise to do much among us. The fact is we are too lazy and unpractical, ourselves, ever to give them much of an idea of that industry and energy which is necessary to form them into men. They will have to go north, where labor is the fashion, the universal custom; and tell me, now, is there enough Christian philanthropy, among your northern states, to bear with the process of their education and elevation? You send thousands of dollars to foreign missions; but could you endure to have the heathens sent into your towns and villages, and give your time, and thoughts, and money, to raise them to the Christian standard? That's what I want to know. If we emancipate, are you willing to educate? How many families in your town would take in a Negro man and woman, teach them, bear with them, and seek to make them Christians? How many merchants would take Adolph, if I wanted to make him a clerk or mechanic, if I wanted him taught a trade? If I wanted to put Jane and Rosa to a school, how many schools are there in the northern states that would

take them in? How many families that would board them? And yet they are as white as many a woman, north or south. You see, Cousin, I want justice done us. We are in a bad position. We are the more obvious oppressors of the Negro; but the unchristian prejudice of the north is an oppressor almost equally severe.

MALALA YOUSAFZAI

There is powerful evidence that the desire to learn is a universal urge among children. Malala Yousafzai was an 11 year old school girl in Pakistan when she took on the Taliban which believes that girls should not go to school. She demanded that girls should be given full access to school. Her campaign led to a blog on the BBC, a New York Times documentary and a Palestinian Peace Prize. She spoke publically many times about her beliefs.

Malala and her friends went to a girls school in Mongora. Since the time of the Taliban, the school had no sign, just an ornamented brass door in a white wall. "For us girls," said Malala, "that doorway was like a magical entrance to our own special world."

As her campaign continued, the Taliban became offended and increasingly angry with Malala and her message. They vowed to kill her. One day when Malala was 15, she was on her way back home after school in a cramped bus carrying 20 girls and 3 teachers. The bus was stopped on the road by two men. One boarded the bus and asked "who is Malala?" Nobody said anything, but several of the girls looked at her. She was the only girl with her face uncovered. The man pulled a pistol and fired three times. The first shot entered her left eye socket and out under her left shoulder. She slumped over and the other two bullets hit two friends sitting next to Malala, one in the shoulder and one in the arm.

Malala was put in a medically induced coma and flown to the Queen Elizabeth Hospital in Birmingham, England. She underwent multiple surgeries and spent nearly 3 months in the hospital which specializes in treating wounded soldiers. Miraculously, the bullet missed her brain and she suffered no major neurological damage. But, the girl's will was solidified: "It feels like this life is not my life. It's a second life. People have prayed to God to spare me and I was spared for a reason—to use my life for helping people."

The Taliban has vowed to try again to kill her so Malala and her family are presently living in England for safety reasons. Malala is enrolled in an all-girls high school. But she continues her campaign. On her 16th Birthday she addressed the United Nations General Assembly urging the delegates to make education a reality for every child around the globe. Malala has become a worldwide celebrity and was nominated for the 2013 Nobel Peace Prize. In April, 2014 she was named by Time Magazine as one of the 100 most influential people in the world.

Because an estimated 57 million school age children in the world get no education, in the fall of 2013, Malala launched the Malala Fund to help girls fight for their education. After all, 70 percent of the people in the world who are living in the poverty are girls and women.

Little Children, Let Us Love

The fight goes on. Although there is no Taliban in Haiti, there is the persistent poverty that affects all school-age children and the continuing tradition and culture of indifference, resistance to the education of girls and the culture of restaveks. Only determination and persistence will change these old habits. The Haitian people must demonstrate that determination and persistence themselves. But they will need some love and a little help.

The plea is summed up by John:

> *"How does God's love abide in anyone who has the world's goods and sees his brother or sister in need and yet refuses to help? Little children, let us love, not in word or speech, but in truth and action."* — 1 John 3: 17, 18

TeacHaiti's mission is to support the education and wellbeing of Haitian children, helping to improve literacy and health in the communities served by TeacHaiti so they may emerge from poverty. TeacHaiti's top priority continues to be developing funding to provide Haitian children and young adults with quality education and improved healthcare within a safe environment.

There are no better words to summarize the case for TeacHaiti than to repeat the statement of Jefferson Laleau, Principal of the School of Hope in an earlier interview:

> We are educating students who will be the leaders of this nation. I see students who will change Haiti. I see doctors, lawyers, technologists, engineers, painters, writers, poets and governmental officials. These are the dreams that we have for our TeacHaiti students. Because of our expectations of them, we are doing the best to train them the best way we know so they can reach their full potential. We want them to be prepared when opportunities are presented.

If you wish to help a little—or a lot, please contact:
TeacHaiti
P.O. Box 1171, Detroit Lakes, MN 56502
Email: miquette@TeacHaiti.org

SALUTE TO JEFF NORBY

"Have not I wept for the one whose life is hard?
Was not my soul grieved for the needy?"

—Job 30: 25

 This book could not have been written without the assistance of Jeff Norby.

It was Jeff who encouraged me to go to Haiti in August of 2010. He organized a six person work crew to go to Port au Prince to paint, fix, furnish and supply the TeacHaiti School of Hope and ready it for the opening of classes the following month. Jeff, along with Tom Klyve, led the workers who included two of Jeff's daughters, Annie and Gretchen, and Melissa Bergman. Jeff's compassion for the Haitian people was palpable and inspiring. A humble leader, Jeff washed the feet of his team at an evening devotional meditation.

It was Jeff who spearheaded my next two trips, in March and December of 2013, to interview Miquette, her family, students, parents, teachers, advisors and supporters of the TeacHaiti program in Port au Prince and St. Michel. He arranged transportation and lodging, was a guide and bodyguard, joined in the interviews, took pictures, asked questions, made suggestions and comments, proofread sections, reviewed drafts and layouts and provided encouraging companionship every step of the way. Jeff Norby is a friend and a rock.

Thank you Jeff for being the indispensable man in this project.

INTERVIEWS

The following persons, listed in alphabetical order, have been interviewed (three by phone) for this book:

Alix, Celene "Vida"

Alix, Roland

Alex, Editte

Audige, Bily

Beneche, Mirna

Cely, Rosemonde

Craft, Dr. William

Dekoter, Tony

Denie, Beatrice

Denie, Chantal

Denie, Cleuis

Denie, Dr. Isaac

Denie, Pidens "Dens"

Denie, Rose

Denie, Sandra

Dols, Joanna

Estebile, Estayan "Tayan"

Ferdin, Rousalyx

Frederickson, Denise

Girault, Passale

Heacock, Dick

Henke, Nancy

Henke, William

Henry, Mario

Hokenstad, Rev. Anne

Jean, Manuel

Jensen, Dr. Clayton

Joseph, Osma

Jules, Daniele

Kilpatrick, Ben

Kilpatrick, Katie

Klyve, Tom

Lee, Cherline

Lee, Farah

Lee, Rev. John

Lee, Mary

MacDonald, Rev. Alan

Marthaler, Vicki

McMahon, Art

McMahon, Miquette Denie

Norby, Jeff

Norby, Michelle

Norvilus, Anouse

Nourry, Pierre

Peterson, Rev. David

Pierre, Claude

Pierre, Justin

Rydell, Dr. Jack

Val, Joseph "Tjoe"

Vilcin, Valentin

White, Julie

ACKNOWLEDGEMENTS

I am so grateful, first of all, to Miquette Denie McMahon for sharing her inspiring story, sharing access to her family, for her hospitality, her patience, her friendship, suggestions and proofreading.

Thanks to John and Mary Lee for the hours and hours sharing family history, photos, letters, clippings, insight, observations, proofreading and corrections. John and Mary have been at the beginning, the middle, every chapter and the ongoing action of this story. They have been generous in so many ways. If it hadn't been for the Lees there would be no TeacHaiti.

Thanks to Tom Klyve, President of TeacHaiti and friend, for his friendly and businesslike approach to this project, his photos, and his guidance on the necessary production steps. Tom and his wife Joyce were also proofreaders with helpful comments, advice and suggestions.

Thanks to board members and local supporters for their interviews, cooperation and encouragement: Vicki Marthaler, Denise Fredrickson, Dick Heacock, Dr. Clayton Jensen, Nancy Henke, Dr. Bill Henke, Michelle Norby and Rev. Dave Peterson. There is a solid "home base" in Detroit Lakes.

Fifty one people have been interviewed for this book for a total of 65 interviews. Thirty one of those were in Haiti. The people of Haiti are so friendly, warm, gracious and encouraging, it was a pleasure to be among them. I thank them sincerely. It is my prayer that this book will in some small way contribute to the growth and education of the children of Haiti.

The hardest working person in this entire project has been our typist, Nancy Kinslow, who with a full time job and two hours of commuting time daily, and starting with a handwritten script, has worked evenings, weekends and probably while everybody else was sleeping to do this manuscript. I have appreciated her hard work, dedication and skills immensely. What a trouper.

Thanks to Teresa Laaveg, Project Manager at Knight Printing for her advice and direction in the assembly and production of this book. She is a creative pro who really cares about her work.

Thanks also to the staff of the Carnegie Public Library in Detroit Lakes for providing private rooms for interviews, reading room space for research and writing and a great atmosphere for thinking, organizing and gathering loose ends.

Not the least of those to thank is my wife, Bev. She has been patient and encouraging. She has overlooked long periods of silence, piles of books and papers, messes and general disorder. She too has proofread sections, asked questions, corrected errors and made helpful suggestions, all with the discipline of a former teacher. Thankfully, she hasn't graded the paper.

John and Mary Lee

SOURCES

Major Sources

Haiti, by Philippe Girard, Palgrave Macmillan (2005, 2010)

Mountains Beyond Mountains, by Tracy Kidder, Random House (2003, 2009)

The Big Truck That Went By, How the World Came To Save Haiti and Left Behind a Disaster, by Jonathan M. Katz, Palgrave Macmillan (2013)

Other Sources

The Stone that the Builder Refused, a novel of Haiti, by Madison Smartt Bell, Random House/Vintage Books (2004)

A History of Latin American from the Beginning to the Present, by Huber Herring, Alfred A. Knopf (1962)

Haiti After the Earthquake, by Paul Farmer, Public Affairs Books (2012)

The Comedians, by Graham Greene, Harper Collins Publishers (1966)

Uncle Tom's Cabin, or *Life Among the Lowly,* by Harriet Beecher Stowe, John P. Jewalty Company (1852)

Why is Haiti so Poor, by Bob Corbett, People to People (1986, 1999)

Haiti's Real Crisis Is Poverty, by Iann Vasques, Daily Laller (2010)

The Lost Children of Haiti, Scott Pelly, CBS News, 60 Minutes

When Helping Hurts, Steve Corbett and Brian Fikkert, Moody Publishers (2009) (How to alleviate poverty without hurting the poor or yourself)

Strength in What Remains, Tracy Kidder, Random House (2009)

Haiti: The U.S. Occupation, 1915-1934, by Christopher Minster, About.com Guide